TABLE OF CONTENTS

Top 15 Test Taking Tips ... 4
Chapter 1 - Whole Numbers ... 5
Chapter 2 - Multiplication and Exponents ... 24
Chapter 3 - Division ... 45
Chapter 4 - Fractions ... 62
Chapter 5 - Decimals ... 79
Chapter 6 - Geometry ... 104
Chapter 7 - Graphs ... 123
Practice Test #1 ... 136
Practice Test #2 ... 151
Thank You ... 169
Online Resources ... 170

Top 15 Test Taking Tips

1. Know the test directions, duration, topics, question types, how many questions
2. Setup a flexible study schedule at least 3-4 weeks before test day
3. Study during the time of day you are most alert, relaxed, and stress free
4. Maximize your learning style; visual learner use visual study aids, auditory learner use auditory study aids
5. Focus on your weakest knowledge base
6. Find a study partner to review with and help clarify questions
7. Practice, practice, practice
8. Get a good night's sleep; don't try to cram the night before the test
9. Eat a well balanced meal
10. Wear comfortable, loose fitting, layered clothing; prepare for it to be either cold or hot during the test
11. Eliminate the obviously wrong answer choices, then guess the first remaining choice
12. Pace yourself; don't rush, but keep working and move on if you get stuck
13. Maintain a positive attitude even if the test is going poorly
14. Keep your first answer unless you are positive it is wrong
15. Check your work, don't make a careless mistake

Chapter 1 - Whole Numbers

Lesson 1

Place Value 1-10,000,000

The place value of a digit is determined by where it is in a number.

Ten Millions	Millions	Hundred Thousands	Ten Thousands	Thousands	Hundreds	Tens	Ones
1	2	3	4	5	6	7	8

12,345,678

Twelve million, three hundred forty-five thousand, six hundred seventy-eight

Match the numbers below to the correct place value boxes.

1. 15,632,782 =

1	5	6	3	2	7	8	2
Ten Millions	Millions	Hundred Thousands	Ten Thousands	Thousands	Hundreds	Tens	Ones

2. 24,879,360 =

Ten Millions	Millions	Hundred Thousands	Ten Thousands	Thousands	Hundreds	Tens	Ones

3. 62,158,524 =

Ten Millions	Millions	Hundred Thousands	Ten Thousands	Thousands	Hundreds	Tens	Ones

4. 30,671,234 =

Ten Millions	Millions	Hundred Thousands	Ten Thousands	Thousands	Hundreds	Tens	Ones

5. 52,197,305 =

Ten Millions	Millions	Hundred Thousands	Ten Thousands	Thousands	Hundreds	Tens	Ones

6. 83,498,147 =

Ten Millions	Millions	Hundred Thousands	Ten Thousands	Thousands	Hundreds	Tens	Ones

Place Value 1-100,000,000

The place value of a digit is determined by where it is in a number.

Hundred Millions	Ten Millions	Millions	Hundred Thousands	Ten Thousands	Thousands	Hundreds	Tens	Ones
1	2	3	4	5	6	7	8	9

123,456,789

One hundred twenty-three million, four hundred fifty-six thousand, seven hundred eighty-nine

Match the numbers below to the correct place value boxes.

1. 748,422,719 =

Hundred Millions	Ten Millions	Millions	Hundred Thousands	Ten Thousands	Thousands	Hundreds	Tens	Ones

2. 329,608,114 =

Hundred Millions	Ten Millions	Millions	Hundred Thousands	Ten Thousands	Thousands	Hundreds	Tens	Ones

3. 124,375,277 =

Hundred Millions	Ten Millions	Millions	Hundred Thousands	Ten Thousands	Thousands	Hundreds	Tens	Ones

4. 741,588,379 =

Hundred Millions	Ten Millions	Millions	Hundred Thousands	Ten Thousands	Thousands	Hundreds	Tens	Ones

5. 504,267,332 =

Hundred Millions	Ten Millions	Millions	Hundred Thousands	Ten Thousands	Thousands	Hundreds	Tens	Ones

6. 972,114,089 =

Hundred Millions	Ten Millions	Millions	Hundred Thousands	Ten Thousands	Thousands	Hundreds	Tens	Ones

Lesson 2

Rounding up to 100,000

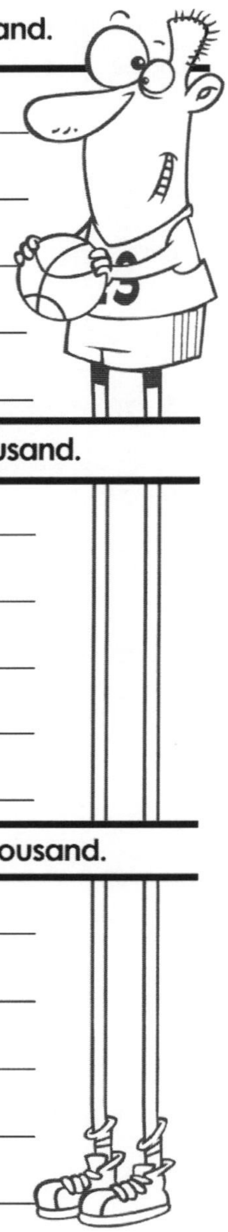

Round the following numbers to the nearest thousand.

1. 2,563 ___3,000___

2. 9,198 ________

3. 1,423 ________

4. 7,712 ________

5. 3,300 ________

6. 4,219 ________

7. 5,756 ________

8. 8,154 ________

9. 6,069 ________

10 1,995 ________

Round the following numbers to the nearest ten-thousand.

11. 39,092 ________

12. 19,917 ________

13. 93,254 ________

14. 56,055 ________

15. 70,856 ________

16. 77,150 ________

17. 33,809 ________

18. 35,451 ________

19. 20,901 ________

20. 48,599 ________

Round the following numbers to the nearest hundred-thousand.

21. 274,333 ________

22. 596,559 ________

23. 221,324 ________

24. 530,708 ________

25. 189,365 ________

26. 317,110 ________

27. 882,658 ________

28. 610,567 ________

29. 789,381 ________

30. 109,277 ________

Lesson 3

Building Numbers

Use what you learned about place value to sort and solve the problems below.

1. 3 + 400 + 4,000 + 20,000 + 50 = 24,453

2. 50,000 + 700 + 10 + 5,000 + 8 = ________

3. 500 + 50 + 10,000 + 9,000 + 4 = ________

4. 8,000 + 100 + 30 + 2 + 20,000 = ________

5. 10,000 + 900 + 60 + 2,000 + 6 = ________

6. 90,000 + 300 + 50 + 9 + 3,000 = ________

7. 1 + 500 + 6,000 + 90,000 + 90 = ________

8. 700 + 70 + 50,000 + 6,000 + 2 = ________

9. 3,000 + 200 + 90 + 7 + 80,000 = ________

10. 5 + 900 + 7,000 + 20,000 + 10 = ________

11. 5,000 + 200 + 10 + 2 + 30,000 = ________

12. 600 + 80 + 60,000 + 2,000 + 9 = ________

13. 40,000 + 200 + 10 + 9,000 + 2 = ________

14. 9,000 + 300 + 50 + 9 + 70,000 = ________

15. 6 + 700 + 3,000 + 90,000 + 50 = ________

16. 8 + 300 + 1,000 + 40,000 + 20 = ________

17. 3,000 + 7 + 50 + 900 + 40,000 = ________

18. 100 + 60 + 10,000 + 4,000 + 1 = ________

19. 500 + 60 + 90,000 + 3,000 + 4 = ________

20. 7 + 800 + 9,000 + 30,000 + 10 = ________

Lesson 4

Estimating 1

To estimate a sum or difference, round each number.
Then add or subtract the rounded numbers.

Addition:

$$\begin{array}{r} 688 \\ +\ 231 \\ \hline \end{array} \longrightarrow \begin{array}{r} 700 \\ +\ 200 \\ \hline 900 \end{array}$$

Subtraction:

$$\begin{array}{r} 4{,}491 \\ -\ 789 \\ \hline \end{array} \longrightarrow \begin{array}{r} 4{,}500 \\ -\ 800 \\ \hline 3{,}700 \end{array}$$

Estimate and solve the problems below.

1. $\begin{array}{r} 858 \\ +\ 391 \\ \hline \end{array} \longrightarrow \begin{array}{r} 900 \\ +\ 400 \\ \hline 1{,}300 \end{array}$

2. $\begin{array}{r} 461 \\ +\ 545 \\ \hline \end{array} \longrightarrow$

3. $\begin{array}{r} 129 \\ +\ 607 \\ \hline \end{array} \longrightarrow$

4. $\begin{array}{r} 399 \\ +\ 731 \\ \hline \end{array} \longrightarrow$

5. $\begin{array}{r} 943 \\ -\ 499 \\ \hline \end{array} \longrightarrow$

6. $\begin{array}{r} 768 \\ -\ 207 \\ \hline \end{array} \longrightarrow$

7. $\begin{array}{r} 630 \\ -\ 452 \\ \hline \end{array} \longrightarrow$

8. $\begin{array}{r} 356 \\ -\ 175 \\ \hline \end{array} \longrightarrow$

Estimating 2

To estimate a sum or difference, round each number. Then add or subtract the rounded numbers.

Estimate and solve the problems below.

1. 6,281 → + 3,552 →	**2.** 4,782 → + 1,321 →	**3.** 9,423 → + 6,599 →
4. 5,192 → + 4,807 →	**5.** 2,991 → + 5,841 →	**6.** 7,510 → + 7,291 →
7. 1,690 → + 4,501 →	**8.** 3,908 → + 4,687 →	**9.** 9,499 → + 532 →
10. 3,641 → - 2,487 →	**11.** 8,961 → - 4,540 →	**12.** 7,299 → - 5,607 →
13. 4,701 → - 3,112 →	**14.** 9,475 → - 7,500 →	**15.** 3,559 → - 1,890 →
16. 4,115 → - 805 →	**17.** 5,602 → - 2,199 →	**18.** 7,999 → - 5,999 →

Lesson 5

Addition with Regrouping

To add multiple-digit numbers together, start in the ones place and then use basic addition rules. When a number equals ten or more the first digit carries over to the next spot. This is called **regrouping**.

Step 1: Add the digits in the one's column and carry over the 1 to the ten's column.

	1000's	100's	10's	1's
			1	
		7	5	9
+		5	6	4
				3

Step 2: Next add the digits in the ten's column and carry over the 1 to the hundred's column.

	1000's	100's	10's	1's
		1	1	
		7	5	9
+		5	6	4
			2	3

Step 3: Next add the digits in the hundred's column.

	1000's	100's	10's	1's
		1	1	
		7	5	9
+		5	6	4
		3	2	3

Step 4: Finally, carry over the 1 from the hundred's column to the thousand's column.

	1000's	100's	10's	1's
		1	1	
		7	5	9
+		5	6	4
	1	3	2	3

Solve the problems below. Use regrouping when needed.

1. 944 + 281 = 1,225

2. 603 + 421

3. 946 + 634

4. 407 + 335

5. 289 + 972

6. 572 + 539

7. 491 + 862

8. 945 + 687

9. 999 + 237

10. 755 + 675

Lesson 6

4-Digit Addition 1

Solve the problems below using regrouping.

1. 1,091 2,157 + 3,267	**2.** 9,815 803 + 2,216	**3.** 3,891 1,259 + 7,520	**4.** 2,552 8,406 + 271
5. 5,330 1,211 + 9,801	**6.** 4,881 2,009 + 1,987	**7.** 3,072 1,650 + 578	**8.** 1,985 8,105 + 1,776
9. 9,841 2,750 + 1,349	**10.** 5,400 501 + 3,814	**11.** 7,072 6,152 + 1,785	**12.** 707 1,804 + 2,950
13. 2,400 962 + 815	**14.** 6,074 1,255 + 8,079	**15.** 8,180 2,755 + 2,577	**16.** 9,064 9,607 + 6,074
17. 4,911 2,757 + 3,025	**18.** 5,787 6,962 + 1,570	**19.** 7,705 5,321 + 1,766	**20.** 3,033 1,447 + 9,632

4-Digit Addition 2

Solve the problems below using regrouping.

1.	**2.**	**3.**	**4.**	**5.**
4,982	5,578	2,121	4,880	6,159
6,350	1,669	9,279	6,524	1,250
9,811	8,902	3,364	9,967	1,975
+ 2,652	+ 191	+ 2,127	+ 2,115	+ 9,364

6.	**7.**	**8.**	**9.**	**10.**
3,160	6,890	2,459	6,110	3,692
9,497	1,457	9,087	993	1,157
5,222	9,058	1,134	1,678	7,239
+ 4,596	+ 3,126	+ 705	+ 5,157	+ 7,058

11.	**12.**	**13.**	**14.**	**15.**
4,457	6,898	3,070	5,158	4,869
9,280	6,157	1,007	4,058	6,048
1,170	3,309	4,911	3,982	9,263
+ 2,357	+ 675	+ 7,963	+ 1,360	+ 2,009

16.	**17.**	**18.**	**19.**	**20.**
1,222	3,089	2,172	3,887	7,982
1,378	6,164	4,339	3,105	3,350
3,157	7,665	6,057	1,007	2,811
+ 9,009	+ 5,035	+ 1,197	+ 332	+ 4,652

Lesson 7

5-Digit Addition

Solve the problems below using regrouping.

1. 54,691 10,847 + 39,116	**2.** 90,861 77,392 + 20,691	**3.** 44,388 35,512 + 64,172	**4.** 50,233 46,397 + 92,846
5. 58,732 33,020 + 12,571	**6.** 19,570 27,694 + 56,630	**7.** 90,691 51,072 + 14,321	**8.** 35,450 82,300 + 23,124
9. 60,805 84,997 + 39,111	**10.** 66,349 70,244 + 11,188	**11.** 15,000 39,289 + 2,723	**12.** 99,785 35,562 + 48,078
13. 38,058 36,298 + 57,613	**14.** 66,951 23,207 + 10,881	**15.** 47,381 61,273 + 75,507	**16.** 94,080 11,636 + 9,860
17. 39,005 29,678 + 14,567	**18.** 48,399 15,467 + 5,005	**19.** 18,222 90,309 + 66,009	**20.** 99,863 99,067 + 65,331

Lesson 8

6-Digit Addition

Solve the problems below using regrouping.

1. 102,220 366,357 + 127,475	**2.** 557,365 166,204 + 254,129	**3.** 325,299 770,351 + 64,658	**4.** 129,195 632,744 + 335,163
5. 641,001 237,925 + 210,137	**6.** 752,112 209,482 + 322,165	**7.** 480,129 638,635 + 218,001	**8.** 500,051 217,521 + 127,937
9. 637,817 289,364 + 123,994	**10.** 491,065 278,605 + 316,221	**11.** 841,316 958,375 + 175,363	**12.** 150,633 534,110 + 156,925
13. 655,119 230,754 + 524,239	**14.** 163,159 952,364 + 402,846	**15.** 752,005 647,119 + 841,715	**16.** 363,175 119,376 + 237,860
17. 445,123 967,525 + 364,129	**18.** 638,117 500,682 + 438,385	**19.** 781,975 237,105 + 285,367	**20.** 908,129 117,765 + 637,032

Lesson 9

7-Digit Addition

Solve the problems below using regrouping.

1. 3,541,277 6,129,245 + 2,382,107	**2.** 2,711,015 3,844,362 + 1,332,745	**3.** 5,008,694 3,992,406 + 8,264,367	**4.** 8,267,200 7,164,245 + 6,277,594
5. 5,466,999 3,050,638 + 6,105,347	**6.** 7,548,007 2,215,635 + 1,365,815	**7.** 9,147,129 6,308,905 + 4,315,707	**8.** 5,113,799 5,564,002 + 6,465,355
9. 1,648,912 3,154,099 + 5,367,474	**10.** 6,905,011 4,322,966 + 3,375,378	**11.** 6,475,619 9,504,242 + 7,289,071	**12.** 1,299,151 3,637,889 + 8,652,234
13. 3,552,910 7,313,577 + 4,429,964	**14.** 6,008,799 5,027,346 + 6,244,310	**15.** 1,224,799 1,496,843 + 9,841,000	**16.** 4,208,577 5,995,685 + 5,372,129
17. 6,141,654 1,764,889 + 7,633,924	**18.** 5,639,047 6,129,885 + 3,445,369	**19.** 9,665,007 8,682,420 + 4,341,204	**20.** 5,245,895 6,636,635 + 8,547,118

Lesson 10

Subtraction with Borrowing

To subtract and borrow, start with the ones column. If the bottom number is of a greater value, you have to borrow from the next column.

Step 1:	**Step 2**:	**Step 3**:	**Step 4**:
Any time the bottom number in a column is of greater value than the top number, you need to borrow.	Borrow 10 from the next column. This reduces the 6 to 5 and increases the number in the first column from 3 to 13.	Now we need to borrow 10 from the hundreds column. This reduces the 7 to 6 and increases the numbers in the tens column from 5 to 15.	Now you are ready for the final step. Finish by subtracting the numbers in all the columns.
100's | 10's | 1's 7 6 3 - 4 8 5	100's | 10's | 1's 5 7 ~~6~~ 13 - 4 8 5	100's | 10's | 1's 6 15 ~~7~~ ~~6~~ 13 - 4 8 5	100's | 10's | 1's 6 15 ~~7~~ ~~6~~ 13 - 4 8 5 2 7 8

Use borrowing to solve the problems below.

1. 682 - 239 443	**2.** 909 - 457	**3.** 342 - 199	**4.** 511 - 227	**5.** 704 - 165
6. 467 - 349	**7.** 919 - 58	**8.** 609 - 158	**9.** 711 - 459	**10.** 197 - 68
11. 679 - 388	**12.** 537 - 87	**13.** 892 - 604	**14.** 906 - 449	**15.** 637 - 205

Lesson 11

4-Digit Subtraction

Use what you learned about borrowing to solve the problems below.

1. 6,432 − 5,320	**2.** 2,675 − 1,564	**3.** 4,233 − 452	**4.** 5,428 − 2,649
5. 1,995 − 239	**6.** 7,321 − 834	**7.** 9,211 − 1,700	**8.** 3,946 − 1,682
9. 2,463 − 1,939	**10.** 8,959 − 3,274	**11.** 1,295 − 968	**12.** 9,942 − 7,895
13. 7,542 − 2,907	**14.** 3,649 − 1,590	**15.** 9,864 − 4,389	**16.** 3,888 − 999
17. 5,001 − 3,547	**18.** 1,775 − 859	**19.** 3,880 − 1,125	**20.** 9,567 − 6,820

Lesson 12

5-Digit Subtraction

Use what you learned about borrowing to solve the problems below.

1. 25,911 - 23,125	**2.** 40,127 - 15,089	**3.** 68,956 - 47,580	**4.** 42,207 - 5,699
5. 30,113 - 9,357	**6.** 92,253 - 75,449	**7.** 57,115 - 36,608	**8.** 21,659 - 17,102
9. 81,678 - 44,169	**10.** 47,827 - 9,018	**11.** 35,157 - 16,658	**12.** 50,011 - 23,956
13. 29,368 - 13,504	**14.** 48,638 - 5,174	**15.** 59,239 - 14,107	**16.** 66,250 - 20,078
17. 36,754 - 18,265	**18.** 54,587 - 33,058	**19.** 63,017 - 5,582	**20.** 92,236 - 15,297

Lesson 13

6-Digit Subtraction

Use what you learned about borrowing to solve the problems below.

1. 627,343	**2.** 854,115	**3.** 506,925	**4.** 129,239
- 495,861	- 346,264	- 229,167	- 95,226
5. 958,062	**6.** 297,343	**7.** 961,343	**8.** 639,447
- 179,687	- 105,907	- 550,097	- 287,334
9. 339,081	**10.** 520,142	**11.** 728,253	**12.** 550,008
- 117,118	- 287,963	- 681,175	- 368,764
13. 785,780	**14.** 902,144	**15.** 811,654	**16.** 495,861
- 358,999	- 751,100	- 436,907	- 399,000
17. 447,675	**18.** 781,115	**19.** 265,017	**20.** 965,305
- 258,007	- 369,098	- 65,336	- 345,999

Lesson 14

7-Digit Subtraction

Use what you learned about borrowing to solve the problems below.

1. 2,135,209 − 1,542,921	**2.** 4,275,394 − 2,866,100	**3.** 6,429,925 − 699,295	**4.** 5,985,324 − 3,547,935
5. 7,122,956 − 5,009,122	**6.** 5,588,133 − 367,794	**7.** 9,002,357 − 1,688,188	**8.** 8,652,116 − 5,775,209
9. 6,339,100 − 3,203,548	**10.** 9,000,142 − 3,872,482	**11.** 7,125,951 − 5,324,007	**12.** 5,689,008 − 1,005,956
13. 9,958,111 − 6,832,504	**14.** 7,194,926 − 2,607,299	**15.** 4,305,842 − 635,184	**16.** 8,965,122 − 5,594,009
17. 6,487,070 − 8,199	**18.** 9,488,267 − 7,129,098	**19.** 6,125,199 − 2.658,037	**20.** 5,600,204 − 3,317,869

Lesson 15

8-Digit Subtraction

Use what you learned about borrowing to solve the problems below.

1. 32,445,311 - 19,306,805	**2.** 54,009,812 - 23,329,605	**3.** 72,511,420 - 49,964,122	**4.** 43,652,019 - 7,994,364
5. 17,457,333 - 9,864,127	**6.** 85,674,152 - 39,200,997	**7.** 55,925,321 - 365,544	**8.** 90,899,425 - 1,621,678
9. 69,129,364 - 34,330,657	**10.** 84,994,657 - 65,732,566	**11.** 88,299,882 - 2,164,295	**12.** 39,599,635 - 10,124,988
13. 67,290,975 - 2,364,963	**14.** 50,400,991 - 6,536,027	**15.** 42,633,635 - 12,396,864	**16.** 95,155,964 - 57,377,337
17. 82,112,650 - 820,941	**18.** 75,644,340 - 38,637,652	**19.** 59,965,122 - 3,637,569	**20.** 93,050,002 - 54,864,632
21. 66,965,362 - 167,064	**22.** 92,338,674 - 17,211,995	**23.** 44,294,632 - 29,009,367	**24.** 84,962,366 - 52,507,999

Chapter 2 - Multiplication and Exponents

Chapter 2 - Multiplication and Exponents

In this chapter you will learn about multiplication and exponents.

Here is what you will learn:

- Multiplication tables
- Multiplying 2-digit numbers
- Multiplying 3-digit numbers
- Multiplying 4-digit numbers
- Multiplying 5-digit numbers
- Understanding Exponents
- Comparing exponents
- Writing exponents

Multiplication Table

x	1	2	3	4	5	6	7	8	9	10
1	1	2	3	4	5	6	7	8	9	10
2	2	4	6	8	10	12	14	16	18	20
3	3	6	9	12	15	18	21	24	27	30
4	4	8	12	16	20	24	28	32	36	40
5	5	10	15	20	25	30	35	40	45	50
6	6	12	18	24	30	36	42	48	54	60
7	7	14	21	28	35	42	49	56	63	70
8	8	16	24	32	40	48	56	64	72	80
9	9	18	27	36	45	54	63	72	81	90
10	10	20	30	40	50	60	70	80	90	100

Lesson 1

Blank Multiplication Table

This is a multiplication table. Multiply the numbers in the top row by the numbers in the side row to get the product.

x	1	2	3	4	5	6	7	8	9	10
1										
2										
3										
4										
5										
6										
7										
8										
9										
10										

Multiplication Table Mix-up

X	1	2	3
1	1	2	3
2	2	4	6

This is a multiplication table. Multiply the numbers in the top row by the numbers in the side row to get the product.

1.

X	4	5	6
6			
5			
4			
3			
2			

2.

X	0	6	8	4	9
5					
4					
3					

3.

X	2	3	4	5	6
10					
11					
12					

4.

X	5	4	3
6			
5			
4			
3			
2			

Lesson 2

Multiplication

To multiply a one-digit number by a two-digit number with regrouping, start in the ones place and then use basic multiplication rules. When the number equals ten or more the first digit carries over to the next spot. This is called **regrouping**.

Step 1: Multiply the numbers in the ones column and carry the first digit over to the tens column.

	Hundreds	Tens	Ones
		2	
		4	7
x			3
			[1]

3 x 7 = 21

Step 2: Multiply the digit in at the bottom of the ones column by the digit in the tens column and add the regrouped number.

	Hundreds	Tens	Ones
		2 +	
		4	7
x			3
		[4]	1

4 x 3 = 12 Then 12 + 2 = 14

Step 3: The one then carries over to the hundreds place.

	Hundreds	Tens	Ones
		2	
		4	7
x			3
	[1]	4	1

Answer = 141

Solve the problems below.

1. 65 x 4 = 260

2. 49 x 3

3. 12 x 9

4. 92 x 6

5. 57 x 8

6. 49 x 8

7. 29 x 4

8. 32 x 5

9. 68 x 7

10. 83 x 9

Lesson 3

Multiplication by 2-Digit Numbers

To multiply a two-digit number by a two-digit number, start in the ones place and then use basic multiplication and addition rules. Don't forget to use what you've learned about regrouping.

1. Multiply by the **ones** multiplier.	2. Multiply by the **tens** multiplier.	3. Add the products.

Hundreds / Tens / Ones
2 (carried)
  4 6
x 2 4
1 8 4
	Hundreds / Tens / Ones
	1 (carried)
	  4 6
	x 2 4
	  1 8 4
	+ 9 2 0
		Hundreds / Tens / Ones
		  4 6
		x 2 4
		  1 8 4
		+ 9 2 0
		1 1 0 4

4 is the first multiplier 4 x 46 = 184	**20 is the second multiplier** 20 x 46 = 104	**Add the two products** 184 + 920 = 1,104

Solve the problems below.

1. 82 x 24 = 328 + 1640 = 1,968

2. 99 x 32

3. 27 x 16

4. 54 x 36

5. 72 x 29

6. 37 x 28

7. 55 x 17

8. 62 x 33

9. 92 x 18

10. 24 x 12

Lesson 4

Multiplying 2-Digit Numbers by 2-Digit Numbers

To multiply a two-digit number by a two-digit number, start in the ones place and then use basic multiplication and addition rules. Dont forget to use what you've learned about regrouping.

Solve the problems below.

1. 49 x 15	**2.** 64 x 24	**3.** 54 x 36	**4.** 67 x 48	**5.** 85 x 65
6. 74 x 46	**7.** 86 x 39	**8.** 35 x 29	**9.** 68 x 47	**10.** 72 x 25
11. 54 x 54	**12.** 87 x 64	**13.** 62 x 43	**14.** 95 x 92	**15.** 42 x 39
16. 96 x 75	**17.** 84 x 15	**18.** 98 x 67	**19.** 76 x 28	**20.** 65 x 57

Lesson 5

Multiplication Word Problems

Use multiplication to solve the problems below.

1. If Tommy plays 7 soccer games, and he blocks 6 shots in each game, how many shots will he block?

2. Larry loves photography and takes a lot of pictures. If he takes 32 pictures a day for 20 days, how many pictures will he take?

3. James is a great painter. He can paint 3 paintings a day. If he paints for 19 days how many paintings will he have?

4. Brian eats pizza every day. If he eats 8 slices a day for 9 days how many slices of pizza will he eat?

Lesson 6

Multiplying 3-Digit Numbers by 2-Digit Numbers 1

To multiply a three-digit number by a two-digit number, start in the ones place and then use basic multiplication and addition rules. Dont forget to use what you've learned about regrouping.

Solve the problems below.

1. 321 x 23

963
+6420
7,383

2. 259 x 19

3. 512 x 43

4. 459 x 36

5. 608 x 25

6. 641 x 39

7. 539 x 62

8. 235 x 24

9. 684 x 31

10. 843 x 64

11. 892 x 83

12. 399 x 95

13. 705 x 34

14. 633 x 79

15. 514 x 92

16. 455 x 99

17. 950 x 64

18. 696 x 82

19. 789 x 34

20. 865 x 96

Multiplying 3-Digit Numbers by 2-Digit Numbers 2

To multiply a three-digit number by a two-digit number, start in the ones place and then use basic multiplication and addition rules. Dont forget to use what you've learned about regrouping.

Solve the problems below.

1. 491 x 52	**2.** 903 x 32	**3.** 384 x 94	**4.** 689 x 17	**5.** 732 x 57
6. 559 x 73	**7.** 197 x 44	**8.** 294 x 54	**9.** 316 x 29	**10.** 917 x 34
11. 827 x 12	**12.** 494 x 37	**13.** 659 x 96	**14.** 749 x 61	**15.** 527 x 72
16. 399 x 57	**17.** 899 x 75	**18.** 421 x 34	**19.** 625 x 84	**20.** 964 x 66

Lesson 7

Multiplication Word Problems 2

Use multiplication to solve the problems below.

1. George has lots of pigs. He keeps 147 pigs in each pen. He has 23 pens. How many pigs does he have in all?

2. Penny is cooking muffins. She can cook 4 muffins per pan. She has 239 pans. How many muffins can she cook?

3. Mickey is going trick or treating. If he goes to 128 houses and collects 12 pieces of candy at each house, how much candy will Mickey have?

4. Nathan is a talented basketball player. If he scores 19 points in each of his next 32 games, how many points will he score?

Lesson 8

Multiplying 4-Digit Numbers by 2-Digit Numbers 1

To multiply a four-digit number by a two-digit number, start in the ones place and then use basic multiplication and addition rules. Don't forget to use what you've learned about regrouping.

Solve the problems below.

1.
$$\begin{array}{r} 1{,}491 \\ \times\ 52 \\ \hline 2982 \\ +\ 74550 \\ \hline 77{,}532 \end{array}$$

2. 6,861 x 15

3. 4,532 x 37

4. 2,725 x 93

5. 3,116 x 29

6. 7,683 x 49

7. 4,492 x 66

8. 2,374 x 97

9. 5,051 x 31

10. 8,790 x 29

11. 2,778 x 86

12. 6,627 x 61

13. 3,055 x 57

14. 6,812 x 89

15. 4,558 x 64

16. 5,109 x 51

17. 9,582 x 75

18. 7,716 x 68

19. 3,337 x 35

20. 8,274 x 59

Multiplying 4-Digit Numbers by 2-Digit Numbers 2

To multiply a four-digit number by a two-digit number, start in the ones place and then use basic multiplication and addition rules. Don't forget to use what you've learned about regrouping.

Solve the problems below.

1. 2,631 × 12	**2.** 3,437 × 20	**3.** 6,115 × 25	**4.** 1,037 × 31	**5.** 4,624 × 29
6. 5,297 × 33	**7.** 1,608 × 37	**8.** 4,809 × 47	**9.** 5,194 × 10	**10.** 3,578 × 36
11. 8,167 × 57	**12.** 5,802 × 66	**13.** 4,950 × 42	**14.** 9,568 × 67	**15.** 7,827 × 74
16. 9,972 × 27	**17.** 5,302 × 37	**18.** 8,185 × 97	**19.** 6,375 × 88	**20.** 9,219 × 96

Lesson 9

Multiplying 3-Digit Numbers by 3-Digit Numbers 1

To multiply a three-digit number by a three-digit number, start in the ones place and then use basic multiplication and addition rules. Don't forget to use what you've learned about regrouping.

Solve the problems below.

1.
```
     432
   x 365
   2,160
  25,920
+129,600
 157,680
```

2. 359 x 619

3. 482 x 165

4. 742 x 363

5. 476 x 134

6. 895 x 135

7. 922 x 617

8. 384 x 475

9. 524 x 277

10. 915 x 674

11. 595 x 186

12. 807 x 132

13. 915 x 337

14. 935 x 476

15. 482 x 982

Multiplying 3-Digit Numbers by 3-Digit Numbers 2

To multiply a three-digit number by a three-digit number, start in the ones place and then use basic multiplication and addition rules. Don't forget to use what you've learned about regrouping.

Solve the problems below.

1. 367 × 182	**2.** 227 × 307	**3.** 521 × 497	**4.** 139 × 927	**5.** 865 × 267
6. 556 × 234	**7.** 682 × 264	**8.** 905 × 114	**9.** 946 × 371	**10.** 568 × 436
11. 637 × 220	**12.** 274 × 369	**13.** 857 × 237	**14.** 475 × 602	**15.** 552 × 189
16. 648 × 422	**17.** 592 × 305	**18.** 200 × 967	**19.** 637 × 137	**20.** 659 × 884

Lesson 10

Multiplying 4-Digit Numbers by 3-Digit Numbers 1

To multiply a four-digit number by a three-digit number, start in the ones place and then use basic multiplication and addition rules. Don't forget to use what you've learned about regrouping.

Solve the problems below.

1. 1,291 x 324 5164 25820 +387300 418,284	**2.** 2,177 x 115	**3.** 4,264 x 137	**4.** 3,387 x 244	**5.** 5,189 x 320
6. 3,654 x 439	**7.** 5,307 x 148	**8.** 2,273 x 259	**9.** 4,892 x 341	**10.** 5,952 x 326
11. 6,489 x 566	**12.** 2,701 x 424	**13.** 3,119 x 178	**14.** 5,297 x 626	**15.** 9,436 x 339
16. 3,624 x 749	**17.** 7,117 x 572	**18.** 5,930 x 897	**19.** 8,175 x 688	**20.** 6,408 x 960

Multiplying 4-Digit Numbers by 3-Digit Numbers 2

To multiply a four-digit number by a three-digit number, start in the ones place and then use basic multiplication and addition rules. Don't forget to use what you've learned about regrouping.

Solve the problems below.

1. 6,584 x 324	**2.** 3,291 x 105	**3.** 8,347 x 137	**4.** 4,551 x 244	**5.** 9,067 x 320
6. 6,561 x 439	**7.** 7,812 x 140	**8.** 3,302 x 259	**9.** 5,191 x 341	**10.** 4,073 x 326
11. 8,651 x 560	**12.** 3,291 x 424	**13.** 5,067 x 682	**14.** 5,297 x 119	**15.** 9,436 x 207
16. 3,624 x 329	**17.** 7,117 x 708	**18.** 5,930 x 132	**19.** 8,175 x 985	**20.** 6,408 x 560

Lesson 11

Exponents 1

An **exponent** is a number that tells how many times the base is used as a factor.
It is written as a smaller number placed above and to the right of the base number.

Example:	Example:
$5^3 = 125$ $(5 \times 5 \times 5) = 125$ 5 is the base number and 3 is the exponent	$3^4 = 81$ $(3 \times 3 \times 3 \times 3) = 81$ 3 is the base number and 4 is the exponent

Write the exponents for each set of numbers.

1. 6 x 6 x 6 x 6 = 6^4

2. 3 x 3 x 3 = _____

3. 5 x 5 x 5 = _____

4. 7 x 7 x 7 x 7 = _____

5. 9 x 9 x 9 x 9 x 9 = _____

6. 8 x 8 x 8 x 8 x 8 x 8 = _____

7. 2 x 2 x 2 x 2 x 2 x 2 = _____

8. 4 x 4 x 4 x 4 = _____

9. 5 x 5 x 5 = _____

10. 6 x 6 x 6 x 6 x 6 = _____

11. 7 x 7 x 7 x 7 x 7 x 7 x 7 = _____

12. 2 x 2 x 2 = _____

13. 3 x 3 x 3 x 3 = _____

14. 9 x 9 x 9 x 9 x 9 x 9 = _____

Lesson 12

Exponents 2

Write out the exponents below and solve. Use the boxes to work out the problems,

1. 9^3 = 9 x 9 x 9 = 729

2. 5^5 = ________________ = ____

3. 8^4 = ________________ = ____

4. 2^9 = ________________ = ____

5. 6^4 = ________________ = ____

6. 4^5 = ________________ = ____

Lesson 13

Exponents 3

Write out the exponents below and solve. Use the boxes to work out the problems,

1. 8^2 = ________________ = ____

2. 6^5 = ________________ = ____

3. 7^4 = ________________ = ____

4. 3^8 = ________________ = ____

5. 4^3 = ________________ = ____

6. 5^5 = ________________ = ____

Comparing Exponents

An **exponent** is a number that tells how many times the base is used as a factor. It is written as a smaller number placed above and to the right of the base number.

Fill in the blanks to answer if each set is greater than, less than or equal.

1. $3^2 \ \boxed{<}\ 2^4$	2. $4^3 \ \square\ 3^2$	3. $2^4 \ \square\ 5^2$
4. $6^5 \ \square\ 4^3$	5. $3^3 \ \square\ 5^2$	6. $5^3 \ \square\ 7^2$
7. $8^4 \ \square\ 5^3$	8. $6^3 \ \square\ 9^3$	9. $4^4 \ \square\ 8^4$
10. $5^2 \ \square\ 9^2$	11. $7^3 \ \square\ 2^2$	12. $4^4 \ \square\ 3^2$
13. $8^3 \ \square\ 4^2$	14. $3^4 \ \square\ 9^3$	15. $6^2 \ \square\ 7^2$

Chapter 3 - Division

In this chapter you will learn about division of large numbers.

Here are the things you will learn:

- Understanding Division
- Division with Remainders
- Division of 2-digit numbers
- Division of 3-digit numbers
- Division of 4-digit numbers
- Division of 5-digit numbers

Division

- Division is a way to find out how many times one number is counted in another number.
- The $\div$ sign means " divided by".
- Use this symbol $\overline{)}$ to set up a division problem.
- The dividend is the larger number that is divided by the smaller number, the divisor.
- The answer of a division problem is called the quotient.

$\div$ is the symbol for division

$$6 \div 2 = 3$$

dividend (6) **divisor** (2) **quotient** (3)

- $6 \div 2 = 3$ is read "6 divided by 2 is equal to 3".
- In $6 \div 2 = 3$, the divisor is 2, the dividend is 6 and the quotient is 3.

$\overline{)}$ is used to divide

$$\begin{array}{r} 5 \\ 2\overline{)10} \end{array}$$

divisor (2) **dividend** (10) **quotient** (5)

- $\begin{array}{r} 5 \\ 2\overline{)10} \end{array}$ is read "10 divided by 2 is equal to 5".
- In $\begin{array}{r} 5 \\ 2\overline{)10} \end{array}$, the divisor is 2, the dividend is 10 and the quotient is 5.

Lesson 1

Division with a 2-Digit Dividend 1

When dividing a **two-digit number** by a **one-digit number**, the quotient can have one or two digits. That is why it is easier to start by breaking the problem down into steps.

Estimate	**Divide the tens**	**Bring down the ones and repeat the steps.**	The answer is: **28 r 1**
2 3)85 Take a look at the first digit. Estimate how many times 3 will go into 8 without going over the number.	2 3)85 - 6 2 3 can go into 8 twice. Multiply 3 x 2 and get 6. Subtract the 6 from 8 leaving 2.	28 3)85 - 6↓ 25 - 24 1 Bring down the 5 from the one's column and repeat the steps. **The remainder is 1**	Remember these steps: **1.** Divide **2.** Multiply **3.** Subtract **4.** Bring down Repeat these steps until there are no more digits to bring down.

Solve these problems. Some may not have remainders.

1. 6)97 = 16 r 1
- 6
37
- 36
1

2. 5)38

3. 7)89

4. 2)91

4. 4)99

6. 3)44

7. 5)58

8. 2)67

Lesson 2

Division with a 2-Digit Dividend 2

Solve these problems. Some may not have remainders.

1. $5\overline{)67}$ **2.** $8\overline{)99}$ **3.** $3\overline{)53}$ **4.** $9\overline{)92}$

5. $2\overline{)78}$ **6.** $7\overline{)80}$ **7.** $5\overline{)73}$ **8.** $3\overline{)64}$

9. $4\overline{)61}$ **10.** $2\overline{)83}$ **11.** $9\overline{)97}$ **12.** $6\overline{)77}$

Lesson 3

Division Word Problems

Use division to solve the problems below.

1. Jerry has 24 boxes to move. He can only carry 3 boxes at a time. How many trips will he have to make to move all the boxes?

2. Sandy has 15 chores to do around the house this week. If she does 3 chores a day, how many days will it take her to do all her chores?

3. Mitchell has 42 apples. He wants to divide them into 6 groups. How many apples will be in each group?

4. Andy has 63 cookies in his jar that he wants to share with his friends. If he has 7 friends, how many cookies will each friend get?

Lesson 4

Dividing 3-Digit Dividends by a 1-Digit Divisor 1

When dividing a larger number by a one-digit number, it is easier to start by breaking the problem down into steps.

Always remember these steps

1. Estimate
2. Divide
3. Multiply
4. Subtract
5. Compare
6. Bring down

Repeat the steps as needed

Here is an example:

Estimate	**Divide the hundreds**	**Bring down the tens and repeat the steps.**	**Bring down the ones and repeat the steps.**
2 4)975	2 4)975 - 8 1	24 4)975 - 8↓ 17 - 16 1	243r3 4)975 - 8 17 - 16↓ 15 - 12 3
Take a look at the first digit. Estimate how many times 4 will go into 9 without going over the number.	4 can go into 9 twice. Multiply 4 x 2 and get 8. Subtract the 8 from 9 leaving 1.	4 can go into 17 four times. Multiply 4 x 4 and get 16. Subtract 16 from 17 leaving 1.	The remainder is **3**

Solve these problems. Some may not have remainders.

1. 367 r 1
2)735
- 6
13
-12
15
- 14
1

2. 3)892

3. 7)938

Lesson 5

Dividing 3-Digit Dividends by a 1-Digit Divisor 2

Solve these problems. Some may not have remainders.

1. $\begin{array}{r} 153r2 \\ 3\overline{)461} \\ -3 \\ \hline 16 \\ -15 \\ \hline 11 \\ -9 \\ \hline 2 \end{array}$

2. $4\overline{)128}$

3. $2\overline{)392}$

4. $7\overline{)975}$

5. $9\overline{)815}$

6. $6\overline{)892}$

7. $3\overline{)564}$

8. $2\overline{)297}$

9. $3\overline{)622}$

10. $4\overline{)930}$

11. $5\overline{)556}$

12. $7\overline{)986}$

13. $2\overline{)846}$

14. $3\overline{)134}$

15. $2\overline{)408}$

16. $2\overline{)276}$

17. $3\overline{)578}$

18. $8\overline{)556}$

19. $9\overline{)681}$

20. $4\overline{)599}$

Dividing 3-Digit Dividends by a 1-Digit Divisor 3

Solve these problems. Some may not have remainders.

1. 9)592	**2.** 5)344	**3.** 7)907	**4.** 2)677	**5.** 6)128
6. 3)750	**7.** 4)417	**8.** 8)982	**9.** 9)337	**10.** 3)827
11. 6)679	**12.** 2)736	**13.** 5)422	**14.** 7)175	**15.** 8)697
16. 9)858	**17.** 2)907	**18.** 4)335	**19.** 9)875	**20.** 5)785

Lesson 6

Dividing 4-Digit Dividends by a 1-Digit Divisor

Solve these problems. Some may not have remainders.

1. $5\overline{)6,207}$

2. $8\overline{)4,557}$

3. $2\overline{)3,045}$

4. $9\overline{)5,671}$

5. $7\overline{)9,278}$

6. $4\overline{)8,715}$

7. $3\overline{)1,896}$

8. $6\overline{)5,809}$

9. $5\overline{)2,254}$

10. $2\overline{)3,735}$

11. $6\overline{)6,854}$

12. $9\overline{)8,994}$

Lesson 7

Dividing 5-Digit Dividends by a 1-Digit Divisor 1

Solve these problems. Some may not have remainders.

1.
```
   8,447r3
4)33,791
 -32
   17
  -16
    19
   -16
     31
    -28
      3
```

2. 3)64,872

3. 6)43,951

4. 2)89,305

5. 7)51,372

6. 5)90,139

7. 9)81,225

8. 3)54,981

9. 4)78,241

10. 7)28,356

11. 6)99,807

12. 9)70,207

Dividing 5-Digit Dividends by 1-Digit Divisor 2

Solve these problems. Some may not have remainders.

1. 9)40,863

2. 6)92,025

3. 8)17,283

4. 7)59,518

5. 2)64,761

6. 5)51,909

7. 3)73,871

8. 8)81,095

9. 6)79,812

10. 4)33,299

11. 9)30,956

12. 7)99,068

Lesson 8

Division Word Problems 2

Use division to solve the problems below.

1. Reggie has 312 letters to deliver. If he delivers 6 letters an hour, how many hours will it take him to deliver all the letters?

2. Suzy is running a marathon. She needs to run 286 miles to finish. She can run 22 miles a day. How many days will it take her to finish the marathon?

3. Ray has 714 square feet of snow to shovel from his yard. He can shovel 14 square feet an hour. How many hours will it take him to shovel all the snow?

4. Dad is building a fence. He has 595 boards. It takes 5 boards to build each section of the fence. How many sections of fence can he make with the boards he has?

Lesson 9

Division with 2-Digit Divisors

When dividing a larger number by a two-digit number, it is easier to start by breaking the problem down into steps.

Here is an example:

Always remember these steps

1. Estimate
2. Divide
3. Multiply
4. Subtract
5. Compare
6. Bring down

Repeat the steps as needed

Estimate	**Divide the first set.**	**Bring down the ones and repeat the steps.**	**Bring the remainder back up top.**
3 24)865	3 24)865 - 72 14	36 24)865 - 72↓ 145 - 144 1	36r1 24)865 - 72↓ 145 - 144 1
Take a look at the first digits. Estimate how many times 24 will go into 86 without going over the number.	24 can go into 86 three times equaling 72. Subtract 72 from 86 leaving 14.	24 can go into 145 six times giving us 144. Subtract 144 from 145 leaving 1.	The remainder is 1

Solve these problems. Some may not have remainders.

1. 31)659 — 21r8
-62
39
- 31
8
2. 46)884
3. 21)429
4. 19)708
5. 38)594
6. 75)999
7. 53)864
8. 60)729
9. 91)963
10. 43)836

Lesson 10

Dividing 3-Digit Dividends by a 2-Digit Divisor

Solve these problems. Some may not have remainders.

1. 12)269 = 22r5 -24 29 -24 5	**2.** 30)738	**3.** 22)449	**4.** 41)209
5. 20)861	**6.** 12)271	**7.** 45)994	**8.** 33)735
9. 35)755	**10.** 11)195	**11.** 29)312	**12.** 63)656
13. 24)681	**14.** 15)575	**15.** 20)468	**16.** 41)630
17. 43)129	**18.** 39)705	**19.** 51)362	**20.** 67)197

Lesson 11

Dividing 4-Digit Dividends by a 2-Digit Divisor

Solve these problems. Some may not have remainders.

1. $13\overline{)2{,}691}$

2. $24\overline{)3{,}558}$

3. $65\overline{)8{,}945}$

4. $54\overline{)6{,}021}$

5. $41\overline{)9{,}278}$

6. $23\overline{)5{,}968}$

7. $36\overline{)7{,}682}$

8. $17\overline{)4{,}950}$

9. $44\overline{)8{,}962}$

10. $16\overline{)1{,}891}$

11. $21\overline{)3{,}398}$

12. $32\overline{)6{,}570}$

Lesson 12

Dividing 5-Digit Dividends by a 2-Digit Divisor 1

Solve these problems. Some may not have remainders.

1. 12)38,756

3,229r8

-36
27
-24
35
-24
116
-108
8

2. 34)85,097

3. 57)96,134

4. 29)64,893

5. 45)95,507

6. 61)35,692

7. 32)96,599

8. 43)77,039

9. 59)32,072

10. 86)90,965

11. 71)80,099

12. 27)43,992

Dividing 5-Digit Dividends by a 2-Digit Divisor 2

Solve these problems. Some may not have remainders.

1. 29)66,126 **2.** 18)40,834 **3.** 43)54,957 **4.** 36)37,993

5. 56)76,013 **6.** 84)99,957 **7.** 70)32,142 **8.** 33)33,962

9. 44)59,195 **10.** 91)85,809 **11.** 62)65,135 **12.** 89)99,066

Chapter 4 - Fractions

Lesson 1

Adding Fractions with Common Denominators

To add fractions with common denominators, just add the numerators. The denominators will remain the same.

Numerators → **Common Denominators** →	$\frac{2}{9} + \frac{3}{9} = \frac{2+3}{9} = \frac{5}{9}$

Add the fractions below.

1. $\frac{6}{15} + \frac{5}{15} + \frac{2}{15} = \frac{13}{15}$

2. $\frac{12}{37} + \frac{7}{37} + \frac{4}{37} =$ ______

3. $\frac{13}{80} + \frac{9}{80} + \frac{27}{80} =$ ______

4. $\frac{8}{109} + \frac{77}{109} + \frac{15}{109} =$ ______

5. $\frac{17}{64} + \frac{3}{64} + \frac{10}{64} =$ ______

6. $\frac{3}{21} + \frac{7}{21} + \frac{4}{21} =$ ______

7. $\frac{205}{865} + \frac{111}{865} + \frac{67}{865} =$ ______

8. $\frac{14}{55} + \frac{8}{55} + \frac{11}{55} =$ ______

9. $\frac{2}{13} + \frac{7}{13} + \frac{1}{13} =$ ______

10. $\frac{2}{74} + \frac{12}{74} + \frac{31}{74} =$ ______

11. $\frac{9}{250} + \frac{140}{250} + \frac{89}{250} =$ ______

12. $\frac{3}{94} + \frac{3}{94} + \frac{1}{94} =$ ______

Lesson 2

Subtracting Fractions with Common Denominators

To subtract fractions with common denominators, just subtract the numerators. The denominators will remain the same.

Numerators →
Common Denominators →

$$\frac{10}{12} - \frac{8}{12} = \frac{10 - 8}{12} = \frac{2}{12}$$

Subtract the fractions below.

1. $\frac{32}{73} - \frac{11}{73} = \frac{21}{73}$

2. $\frac{12}{28} - \frac{5}{28} =$ ____

3. $\frac{78}{89} - \frac{56}{89} =$ ____

4. $\frac{112}{146} - \frac{92}{146} =$ ____

5. $\frac{233}{634} - \frac{119}{634} =$ ____

6. $\frac{8}{12} - \frac{4}{12} =$ ____

7. $\frac{608}{759} - \frac{325}{759} =$ ____

8. $\frac{45}{56} - \frac{19}{56} =$ ____

9. $\frac{178}{207} - \frac{99}{207} =$ ____

10. $\frac{30}{49} - \frac{17}{49} =$ ____

11. $\frac{246}{277} - \frac{79}{277} =$ ____

12. $\frac{439}{534} - \frac{201}{534} =$ ____

13. $\frac{77}{88} - \frac{11}{88} =$ ____

14. $\frac{68}{129} - \frac{29}{129} =$ ____

15. $\frac{894}{952} - \frac{705}{952} =$ ____

Lesson 3

Fraction Word Problems

Write the correct fractions for each question below.

1. Daryl is working on his garden. He has planted 28 plants so far. He has 13 tomato plants, 6 eggplants and 9 potato plants. Write the fraction that represents each type of plant.

Tomatoes: $\frac{13}{28}$ **Eggplants:** $\frac{6}{28}$ **Potatoes:** $\frac{9}{28}$

2. Mom's favorite hobby is bird watching. Today she saw 15 different birds. She saw 3 blue jays, 9 sparrows, 6 ducks and 1 eagle. Write the fraction that represents each set of birds.

Blue Jays: ______ **Sparrows:** ______ **Ducks:** ______ **Eagles:** ______

3. Johnny went fishing today and caught 17 fish. He caught 2 bass, 6 trout, 5 guppies and 4 goldfish. Write the fraction that represents each type of fish.

Bass: ______ **Trout:** ______ **Guppies:** ______ **Goldfish:** ______

4. Dad is barbequing for the party this afternoon. He has 76 items to cook. He is going to cook 15 hamburgers, 22 chicken wings and 39 sausages.

Hamburgers: ______ **Chicken Wings:** ______ **Sausages:** ______

Lesson 4

Equivalent Fractions

Equivalent Fractions are fractions that have the same value. Even though each shape is divided into a different amount of parts, the shaded parts are equal.

$\frac{2}{4}$ of the circle is shaded in. 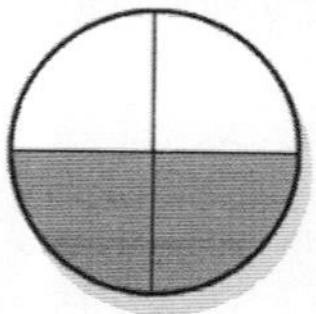

$\frac{4}{8}$ of the circle is shaded in. 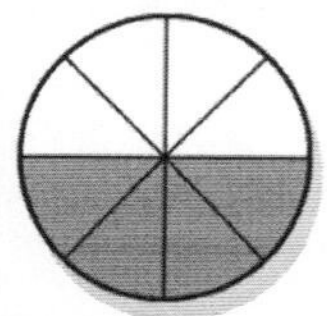

$\frac{2}{4}$ and $\frac{4}{8}$ are equivalent fractions. $\frac{2}{4} = \frac{4}{8}$

Shade in the equivalent fractions on the right to equal the fractions on the left.

$\frac{1}{4}$ 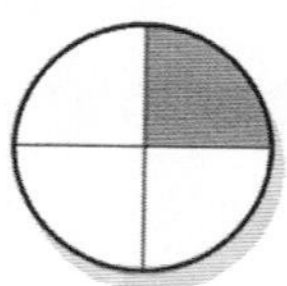 $=$ $\frac{2}{8}$ 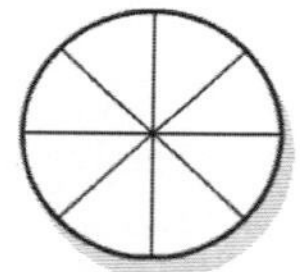

$\frac{2}{4}$ 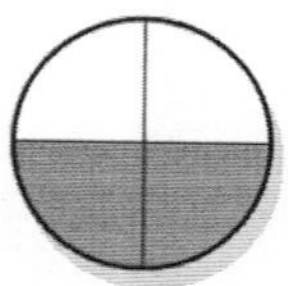 $=$ $\frac{4}{8}$ 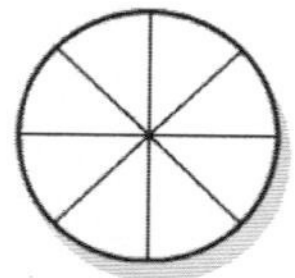

$\frac{3}{8}$ 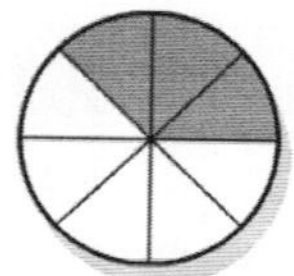 $=$ $\frac{6}{16}$ 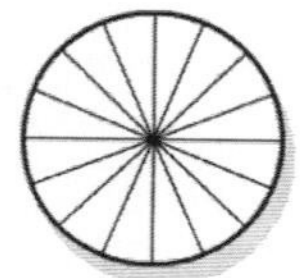

$\frac{5}{8}$ 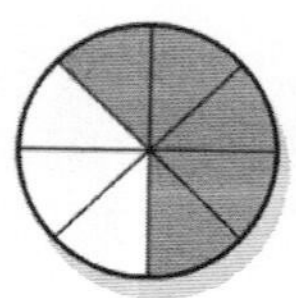 $=$ $\frac{10}{16}$ 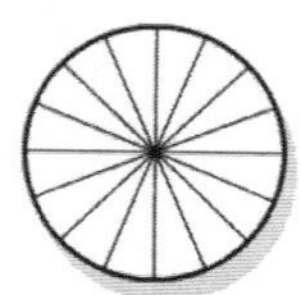

Lesson 5

Reducing to Equivalent Fractions

- Reducing (or simplifying) fractions means reducing a fraction to an equivalent fraction that has the smallest possible numbers.
- To do this, find the largest number that both the numerator and denominator are divisible by. Then divide both by that number.

Example 1:	Example 2:
$\frac{15}{21} \div \left[\frac{3}{3}\right] = \frac{5}{7}$ $\frac{15}{21} = \frac{5}{7}$	$\frac{12}{20} \div \left[\frac{4}{4}\right] = \frac{3}{5}$ $\frac{12}{20} = \frac{3}{5}$

Reduce the fractions to lowest terms.

1. $\frac{18}{27} \div \frac{9}{9} = \frac{2}{3}$

2. $\frac{4}{12} \div \frac{\quad}{\quad} = \frac{\quad}{\quad}$

3. $\frac{20}{35} \div \frac{\quad}{\quad} = \frac{\quad}{\quad}$

4. $\frac{9}{24} \div \frac{\quad}{\quad} = \frac{\quad}{\quad}$

5. $\frac{15}{21} \div \frac{\quad}{\quad} = \frac{\quad}{\quad}$

6. $\frac{16}{40} \div \frac{\quad}{\quad} = \frac{\quad}{\quad}$

7. $\frac{10}{25} \div \frac{\quad}{\quad} = \frac{\quad}{\quad}$

8. $\frac{16}{36} \div \frac{\quad}{\quad} = \frac{\quad}{\quad}$

9. $\frac{12}{30} \div \frac{\quad}{\quad} = \frac{\quad}{\quad}$

10. $\frac{9}{27} \div \frac{\quad}{\quad} = \frac{\quad}{\quad}$

11. $\frac{8}{14} \div \frac{\quad}{\quad} = \frac{\quad}{\quad}$

12. $\frac{16}{32} \div \frac{\quad}{\quad} = \frac{\quad}{\quad}$

Lesson 6

Reducing to Equivalent Fractions with Common Denominators

Before we can add or subtract fractions, we must make sure they have common denominators. There are two ways to do this–using multiplication or division. Let's look at division first.

$$\frac{9}{12} - \frac{1}{4}$$

In order to subtract these fractions, we must change one to an equivalent fraction with a common denominator (in this case, 4). To change a fraction to an equivalent fraction, divide the numerator and the denominator by the same number (in this case, 3).

Numerator → 9
Denominator → 12

$$\frac{9}{12} = \frac{9 \div 3}{12 \div 3} = \frac{3}{4}$$

$\frac{1}{4}$ and $\frac{3}{4}$ now have common denominators.

Example: Before we can find the difference, we must find an equivalent fraction with a common denominator.

Change this: $\frac{9}{12} - \frac{1}{4}$ = **To this & subtract:** $\frac{3}{4} - \frac{1}{4} = \frac{2}{4}$

1. $\frac{6}{10} + \frac{1}{5} = \frac{3}{5} + \frac{1}{5} = \frac{4}{5}$

2. $\frac{8}{12} + \frac{1}{6} = \underline{\quad} + \frac{1}{6} = \underline{\quad}$

3. $\frac{9}{21} + \frac{2}{7} = \underline{\quad} + \frac{2}{7} = \underline{\quad}$

4. $\frac{12}{32} + \frac{3}{8} = \underline{\quad} + \frac{3}{8} = \underline{\quad}$

5. $\frac{15}{25} - \frac{1}{5} = \underline{\quad} - \frac{1}{5} = \underline{\quad}$

6. $\frac{15}{20} - \frac{1}{4} = \underline{\quad} - \frac{1}{4} = \underline{\quad}$

7. $\frac{25}{35} - \frac{3}{7} = \underline{\quad} - \frac{3}{7} = \underline{\quad}$

8. $\frac{32}{36} - \frac{4}{9} = \underline{\quad} - \frac{4}{9} = \underline{\quad}$

Lesson 7

Adding Fractions with Different Denominators - Using Division

To add fractions with different denominators, first find a common denominator. Then add the numerators.

Solve each problem. Find each common denominator and sum.

1. $\frac{15}{21} = \frac{5}{7}$; $+\ \frac{2}{7} = +\ \frac{2}{7}$; sum: $\frac{7}{7}$

2. $\frac{1}{5} = \frac{\quad}{\quad}$; $+\ \frac{8}{20} = +\ \frac{\quad}{\quad}$; sum: $\frac{\quad}{\quad}$

3. $\frac{21}{30} = \frac{\quad}{\quad}$; $+\ \frac{2}{10} = +\ \frac{\quad}{\quad}$; sum: $\frac{\quad}{\quad}$

4. $\frac{10}{12} = \frac{\quad}{\quad}$; $+\ \frac{6}{36} = +\ \frac{\quad}{\quad}$; sum: $\frac{\quad}{\quad}$

5. $\frac{2}{9} = \frac{\quad}{\quad}$; $+\ \frac{18}{54} = +\ \frac{\quad}{\quad}$; sum: $\frac{\quad}{\quad}$

6. $\frac{25}{35} = \frac{\quad}{\quad}$; $+\ \frac{2}{7} = +\ \frac{\quad}{\quad}$; sum: $\frac{\quad}{\quad}$

7. $\frac{54}{81} = \frac{\quad}{\quad}$; $+\ \frac{1}{9} = +\ \frac{\quad}{\quad}$; sum: $\frac{\quad}{\quad}$

8. $\frac{27}{36} = \frac{\quad}{\quad}$; $+\ \frac{2}{12} = +\ \frac{\quad}{\quad}$; sum: $\frac{\quad}{\quad}$

9. $\frac{6}{7} = \frac{\quad}{\quad}$; $+\ \frac{28}{49} = +\ \frac{\quad}{\quad}$; sum: $\frac{\quad}{\quad}$

10. $\frac{56}{64} = \frac{\quad}{\quad}$; $+\ \frac{1}{8} = +\ \frac{\quad}{\quad}$; sum: $\frac{\quad}{\quad}$

11. $\frac{3}{9} = \frac{\quad}{\quad}$; $+\ \frac{20}{36} = +\ \frac{\quad}{\quad}$; sum: $\frac{\quad}{\quad}$

12. $\frac{81}{90} = \frac{\quad}{\quad}$; $+\ \frac{7}{10} = +\ \frac{\quad}{\quad}$; sum: $\frac{\quad}{\quad}$

Lesson 8

Subtracting Fractions with Different Denominators - Using Division

To add fractions with different denominators, first find a common denominator. Then add the numerators.

Solve each problem. Find each common denominator and sum.

1. $\frac{12}{18} = \frac{12}{18}$ $\quad - \frac{2}{9} = \frac{4}{18}$ $\quad \frac{8}{18}$

2. $\frac{4}{7} = \_\_$ $\quad - \frac{3}{21} = \_\_$ $\quad \_\_$

3. $\frac{7}{9} = \_\_$ $\quad - \frac{20}{45} = \_\_$ $\quad \_\_$

4. $\frac{28}{35} = \_\_$ $\quad - \frac{3}{5} = \_\_$ $\quad \_\_$

5. $\frac{3}{7} = \_\_$ $\quad - \frac{18}{63} = \_\_$ $\quad \_\_$

6. $\frac{36}{42} = \_\_$ $\quad - \frac{5}{7} = \_\_$ $\quad \_\_$

7. $\frac{81}{81} = \_\_$ $\quad - \frac{6}{9} = \_\_$ $\quad \_\_$

8. $\frac{8}{9} = \_\_$ $\quad - \frac{12}{36} = \_\_$ $\quad \_\_$

9. $\frac{6}{7} = \_\_$ $\quad - \frac{21}{49} = \_\_$ $\quad \_\_$

10. $\frac{8}{9} = \_\_$ $\quad - \frac{12}{54} = \_\_$ $\quad \_\_$

11. $\frac{5}{6} = \_\_$ $\quad - \frac{16}{48} = \_\_$ $\quad \_\_$

12. $\frac{32}{36} = \_\_$ $\quad - \frac{5}{9} = \_\_$ $\quad \_\_$

Lesson 9

Finding Common Denominators using Multiplication 1

Before we can add or subtract fractions, we must make sure they have common denominators. There are two ways to do this–using multiplication or division. Let's look at multiplication .

To change a fraction to an equivalent fraction, multiply the numerator and the denominator by the same number.

Example: Before we can add these fractions we must find a common denominator.

Change this: $\frac{2}{6} + \frac{2}{12}$ = **To this & add:** $\frac{4}{12} + \frac{2}{12} = \frac{6}{12}$

Numerator → / Denominator → $\frac{2}{6} = \frac{2 \times 2}{6 \times 2} = \frac{4}{12}$

$\frac{2}{12}$ and $\frac{4}{12}$ now have a common denominator.

Fill in the blanks to complete the equivalent fractions.

1. $\frac{2}{6} \times \frac{2}{2} = \frac{4}{12}$
2. $\frac{3}{5} \times \frac{\quad}{\quad} = \frac{9}{15}$
3. $\frac{6}{8} \times \frac{\quad}{\quad} = \frac{24}{32}$
4. $\frac{5}{7} \times \frac{\quad}{\quad} = \frac{15}{21}$
5. $\frac{2}{3} \times \frac{\quad}{\quad} = \frac{16}{24}$
6. $\frac{3}{4} \times \frac{\quad}{\quad} = \frac{15}{20}$
7. $\frac{3}{7} \times \frac{\quad}{\quad} = \frac{9}{21}$
8. $\frac{2}{6} \times \frac{\quad}{\quad} = \frac{22}{66}$
9. $\frac{2}{6} \times \frac{\quad}{\quad} = \frac{18}{54}$

Lesson 10

Finding Common Denominators Using Multiplication 2

- We just learned that one way to find **equivalent fractions** is to multiply both the numerator and denominator by the same number.
- So this means $\frac{2}{6} = \frac{4}{12}$

$$\frac{2}{6} = \frac{2 \times 2}{6 \times 2} = \frac{4}{12} \begin{matrix} \leftarrow \text{Numerator} \\ \leftarrow \text{Denominator} \end{matrix}$$

$\frac{2}{6}$ and $\frac{4}{12}$ are now **equivalent fractions**.

Fill in the blanks to make the fractions below equivalent fractions.

1. $\frac{3}{5} = \frac{\_\_}{20}$	**2.** $\frac{2}{4} = \frac{6}{\_\_}$	**3.** $\frac{1}{2} = \frac{\_\_}{20}$	**4.** $\frac{6}{8} = \frac{30}{\_\_}$
5. $\frac{1}{7} = \frac{\_\_}{35}$	**6.** $\frac{2}{6} = \frac{30}{\_\_}$	**7.** $\frac{4}{5} = \frac{\_\_}{100}$	**8.** $\frac{2}{4} = \frac{\_\_}{32}$
9. $\frac{4}{12} = \frac{\_\_}{84}$	**10.** $\frac{5}{10} = \frac{45}{\_\_}$	**11.** $\frac{3}{7} = \frac{6}{\_\_}$	**12.** $\frac{3}{5} = \frac{33}{\_\_}$
13. $\frac{9}{16} = \frac{72}{\_\_}$	**14.** $\frac{1}{3} = \frac{\_\_}{45}$	**15.** $\frac{15}{25} = \frac{30}{\_\_}$	**16.** $\frac{16}{18} = \frac{\_\_}{90}$
17. $\frac{3}{16} = \frac{\_\_}{64}$	**18.** $\frac{3}{5} = \frac{\_\_}{25}$	**19.** $\frac{4}{6} = \frac{4}{\_\_}$	**20.** $\frac{2}{8} = \frac{4}{\_\_}$

Lesson 11

Adding Fractions with Different Denominators - Using Multiplication

To change a fraction to an equivalent fraction, multiply the numerator and the denominator by the same number.

Fill in the blanks to find equivalent fractions, then add the fractions.

1. $\frac{2}{4} = \frac{4}{8}$, $+\frac{1}{8} = +\frac{1}{8}$, total: $\frac{5}{8}$

2. $\frac{4}{12} = \frac{\_\_}{12}$, $+\frac{3}{6} = +\frac{\_\_}{12}$, total: $\frac{\_\_}{\_\_}$

3. $\frac{2}{7} = \frac{\_\_}{21}$, $+\frac{5}{21} = +\frac{\_\_}{21}$, total: $\frac{\_\_}{\_\_}$

4. $\frac{4}{28} = \frac{\_\_}{28}$, $+\frac{3}{4} = +\frac{\_\_}{28}$, total: $\frac{\_\_}{\_\_}$

5. $\frac{3}{5} = \frac{\_\_}{50}$, $+\frac{12}{50} = +\frac{\_\_}{50}$, total: $\frac{\_\_}{\_\_}$

6. $\frac{6}{24} = \frac{\_\_}{24}$, $+\frac{5}{8} = +\frac{\_\_}{24}$, total: $\frac{\_\_}{\_\_}$

7. $\frac{21}{48} = \frac{\_\_}{48}$, $+\frac{2}{6} = +\frac{\_\_}{48}$, total: $\frac{\_\_}{\_\_}$

8. $\frac{5}{9} = \frac{\_\_}{81}$, $+\frac{12}{81} = +\frac{\_\_}{81}$, total: $\frac{\_\_}{\_\_}$

9. $\frac{9}{36} = \frac{\_\_}{36}$, $+\frac{3}{6} = +\frac{\_\_}{36}$, total: $\frac{\_\_}{\_\_}$

10. $\frac{4}{9} = \frac{\_\_}{63}$, $+\frac{5}{63} = +\frac{\_\_}{63}$, total: $\frac{\_\_}{\_\_}$

11. $\frac{39}{72} = \frac{\_\_}{72}$, $+\frac{3}{9} = +\frac{\_\_}{72}$, total: $\frac{\_\_}{\_\_}$

12. $\frac{17}{56} = \frac{\_\_}{56}$, $+\frac{5}{8} = +\frac{\_\_}{56}$, total: $\frac{\_\_}{\_\_}$

Lesson 12

Subtracting Fractions with Different Denominators - Using Multiplication

To change a fraction to an equivalent fraction, multiply the numerator and the denominator by the same number.

Fill in the blanks to find equivalent fractions, then subtract.

1.
$$\frac{2}{4} = \frac{10}{20}$$
$$-\frac{6}{20} = -\frac{6}{20}$$
$$\frac{4}{20}$$

2.
$$\frac{14}{15} = \frac{\_\_}{15}$$
$$-\frac{4}{5} = -\frac{\_\_}{15}$$
$$\_\_$$

3.
$$\frac{13}{18} = \frac{\_\_}{18}$$
$$-\frac{2}{6} = -\frac{\_\_}{18}$$
$$\_\_$$

4.
$$\frac{35}{40} = \frac{\_\_}{40}$$
$$-\frac{2}{4} = -\frac{\_\_}{40}$$
$$\_\_$$

5.
$$\frac{5}{6} = \frac{\_\_}{48}$$
$$-\frac{29}{48} = -\frac{\_\_}{48}$$
$$\_\_$$

6.
$$\frac{16}{24} = \frac{\_\_}{24}$$
$$-\frac{5}{8} = -\frac{\_\_}{24}$$
$$\_\_$$

7.
$$\frac{36}{49} = \frac{\_\_}{49}$$
$$-\frac{3}{7} = -\frac{\_\_}{49}$$
$$\_\_$$

8.
$$\frac{5}{6} = \frac{\_\_}{54}$$
$$-\frac{29}{54} = -\frac{\_\_}{54}$$
$$\_\_$$

9.
$$\frac{63}{81} = \frac{\_\_}{81}$$
$$+\frac{6}{9} = -\frac{\_\_}{81}$$
$$\_\_$$

10.
$$\frac{54}{63} = \frac{\_\_}{63}$$
$$-\frac{5}{9} = -\frac{\_\_}{63}$$
$$\_\_$$

11.
$$\frac{27}{48} = \frac{\_\_}{48}$$
$$-\frac{4}{8} = -\frac{\_\_}{48}$$
$$\_\_$$

12.
$$\frac{35}{50} = \frac{\_\_}{100}$$
$$-\frac{50}{100} = -\frac{\_\_}{100}$$
$$\_\_$$

Lesson 13

Mixed Numbers with Common Denominators

When we add or subtract mixed numbers with common denominators, we need to first add or subtract the fractions. Next add or subtract the whole numbers.

Example 1: $2\frac{2}{8} + 6\frac{3}{8}$

Step 1: Add the fractions

$$\begin{array}{r} 2\frac{2}{8} \\ +6\frac{3}{8} \\ \hline \frac{5}{8} \end{array}$$

Step 2: Add the whole numbers

$$\begin{array}{r} 2\frac{2}{8} \\ +6\frac{3}{8} \\ \hline 8\frac{5}{8} \end{array}$$

Example 2: $5\frac{9}{12} - 3\frac{5}{12}$

Step 1: Subtract the fractions

$$\begin{array}{r} 5\frac{9}{12} \\ -3\frac{5}{12} \\ \hline \frac{4}{12} \end{array}$$

Step 2: Subtract the whole numbers

$$\begin{array}{r} 5\frac{9}{12} \\ -3\frac{5}{12} \\ \hline 2\frac{4}{12} \end{array}$$

Add or subtract the mixed numbers below.

1. $3\frac{6}{12} + 2\frac{4}{12} = 5\frac{10}{12}$

2. $5\frac{3}{9} + 1\frac{1}{9}$

3. $4\frac{2}{5} + 3\frac{2}{5}$

4. $1\frac{8}{23} + 1\frac{12}{23}$

5. $9\frac{2}{8} + 4\frac{4}{8}$

6. $6\frac{3}{15} + 7\frac{7}{15}$

7. $8\frac{21}{39} + 5\frac{9}{39}$

8. $3\frac{4}{10} + 9\frac{5}{10}$

9. $6\frac{12}{19} - 2\frac{7}{19}$

10. $8\frac{7}{8} - 5\frac{2}{8}$

11. $10\frac{14}{16} - 7\frac{8}{16}$

12. $14\frac{5}{6} - 9\frac{1}{6}$

13. $24\frac{21}{25} - 19\frac{17}{25}$

14. $36\frac{9}{10} - 25\frac{8}{10}$

15. $46\frac{39}{44} - 38\frac{12}{44}$

Lesson 14

Reducing Mixed Numbers with Common Denominators

- When we add or subtract mixed numbers with common denominators, first we need to add or subtract the fractions. Next add or subtract the whole numbers.
- When reducing, remember to divide by the largest number possible.

Add or subtract the mixed numbers below, then reduce to the simplest form.

1. $4\frac{3}{10} + 1\frac{2}{10}$

   $5\frac{5}{10} = 5\frac{1}{2}$

2. $4\frac{8}{12} + 5\frac{1}{12}$

3. $3\frac{2}{18} + 6\frac{4}{18}$

4. $3\frac{1}{8} + 5\frac{3}{8}$

5. $7\frac{7}{24} + 5\frac{5}{24}$

6. $9\frac{10}{36} + 6\frac{8}{36}$

7. $4\frac{5}{56} + 7\frac{16}{56}$

8. $8\frac{22}{81} + 6\frac{23}{81}$

9. $12\frac{10}{16} - 9\frac{2}{16}$

10. $17\frac{5}{12} - 5\frac{1}{12}$

11. $11\frac{21}{28} - 3\frac{7}{28}$

12. $29\frac{9}{9} - 17\frac{3}{9}$

13. $48\frac{37}{42} - 9\frac{9}{42}$

14. $72\frac{25}{63} - 54\frac{7}{63}$

15. $50\frac{18}{21} - 25\frac{6}{21}$

16. $36\frac{32}{50} - 25\frac{12}{50}$

Lesson 15

Converting Mixed Numbers

To add, subtract, multiply or divide mixed numbers by other fractions, we need to convert the mixed number to an improper fraction.

Step 1:	Step 2:	Step 3:
Multiply the whole number by the denominator.	Add the numerator to the product.	Keep the denominator the same.
$2\frac{1}{4} = \frac{2 \times 4}{4}$	$2\frac{1}{4} = \frac{2 \times 4 + 1}{4} = \frac{9}{4}$	$2\frac{1}{4} = \frac{9}{4}$

Convert each mixed number to an improper fraction.

1. $3\frac{4}{3} = \frac{13}{3}$
2. $8\frac{6}{4} =$ ___
3. $2\frac{9}{2} =$ ___
4. $6\frac{2}{5} =$ ___
5. $9\frac{5}{10} =$ ___
6. $4\frac{1}{5} =$ ___
7. $3\frac{4}{7} =$ ___
8. $1\frac{11}{3} =$ ___
9. $5\frac{1}{5} =$ ___
10. $8\frac{6}{3} =$ ___
11. $4\frac{7}{5} =$ ___
12. $2\frac{2}{8} =$ ___
13. $9\frac{7}{5} =$ ___
14. $7\frac{6}{3} =$ ___
15. $6\frac{3}{11} =$ ___
16. $3\frac{7}{3} =$ ___
17. $1\frac{15}{22} =$ ___
18. $2\frac{6}{9} =$ ___
19. $8\frac{2}{4} =$ ___
20. $9\frac{5}{3} =$ ___

Lesson 16

Improper Fractions

Improper fractions are fractions that have a numerator greater than or equal to the denominator.

Numerator → $\frac{8}{8}, \frac{49}{7}, \frac{10}{5}$ ← Denominator

To convert an **improper fraction** into a whole number or mixed number, divide the numerator by the denominator.

$\frac{8}{8} = 8\overline{)8}$ = 1 $\qquad$ $\frac{49}{7} = 7\overline{)49}$ = 7

$\frac{10}{5} = 5\overline{)10}$ = 2

When converting improper fractions, sometimes you get remainders. This means you will get **mixed numbers**. Write the remainder as a fraction with the divisor as the bottom number.

$\frac{9}{5} = 5\overline{)9}$ = $2\frac{1}{5}$

-8

1

Convert the fractions below.

Convert these fractions to whole numbers:

1. $\frac{35}{5} = 7$ $\qquad$ **2.** $\frac{12}{3} =$ ____ $\qquad$ **3.** $\frac{24}{8} =$ ____ $\qquad$ **4.** $\frac{27}{3} =$ ____

5. $\frac{48}{6} =$ ____ $\qquad$ **6.** $\frac{93}{3} =$ ____ $\qquad$ **7.** $\frac{25}{5} =$ ____ $\qquad$ **8.** $\frac{84}{2} =$ ____

Convert these fractions to mixed numbers:

9. $\frac{15}{6} = 2\frac{3}{6}$ $\qquad$ **10.** $\frac{10}{4} =$ ____ $\qquad$ **11.** $\frac{7}{2} =$ ____ $\qquad$ **12.** $\frac{19}{8} =$ ____

13. $\frac{23}{4} =$ ____ $\qquad$ **14.** $\frac{26}{3} =$ ____ $\qquad$ **15.** $\frac{50}{9} =$ ____ $\qquad$ **16.** $\frac{46}{8} =$ ____

Chapter 5 - Decimals

In this chapter you will learn about decimals and how they relate to money. **Here are the things you will learn:**

- Lining up Decimals
- Addition of Decimals
- Subtraction of Decimals
- Addition and Subtraction of Money

Lesson 1

Decimal Points Addition

Adding decimals is like most normal addition. You just have to remember to line up the decimals.

Hint: Decimal points always go at the end of a whole number (3 = 3.0 or 3.00)

Example: Add 6.33, 5 and 9.5

Step 1: Line up the numbers	**Step 2:** Add zeros	**Step 3:** Find the total
6.33	6.33	6.33
5.	5.00	5.00
+ 9.5	+ 9.50	+ 9.50
		20.83

Line up the numbers and solve the problems below.
Show your work in the boxes.

1: 5.84 + 1.7 + 3.29

$$\begin{array}{r} 5.84 \\ 1.70 \\ +\ 3.29 \\ \hline 10.83 \end{array}$$

2: 8.09 + 2.97 + .49

3: 6.94 + 3.07 + 7

4: 24 + 11.09 + 39.74

5: 70.05 + .95 + .38

6: 9.99 + .83 + 60.4

Lesson 2

Arranging and Adding Decimals 1

Use what you learned about adding numbers with decimals to find the totals to the questions below. Show your work in the boxes.

1: 10.54 + 8.01 + .89

2: 6.32 + 9.51 + 1.99

3: .99 + 5.15 + 12.47

4: 4.21 + 3.57 + 15.05

5: 11.97 + 246.1 + 6.50

6: .23 + 13.31 + 72.08

7: 61.59 + 31.64 + .08

8: 84 + 16.99 + 14.89

9: 8.50 + 7.27 + 985

Arranging and Adding Decimals 2

Use what you learned about adding numbers with decimals to find the totals to the questions below. Show your work in the boxes.

1: .154 + 28.46 + 11.751

2: 9.81 + .011 + 6.907

3: 3.645 + 5.707 + 99

4: 6.59 + 1.194 + 5.99

5: 29.175 + 35.19 + 3.809

6: 1.567 + 88.09 + 41.78

7: 58.079 + 44.015 + 7.09

8: 1.955 + 44.19 + 70.091

9: 9.89 + .275 + 67.001

Arranging and Adding Decimals 3

Use what you learned about adding numbers with decimals to find the totals to the questions below. Show your work in the boxes.

1: 164.99 + 805.46 + .75

2: 150.92 + 321 + 50.24

3: 95.56 + 128.7 + 9.23

4: 389.04 + 84.99 + 6.15

5: 18.56 + 991.5 + 525.09

6: 61.91 + 571.17 + 223.09

7: 7.56 + 75.61 + 756.1

8: 395.1 + 395.11 + 39.51

9: 91.8 + 9.18 + 918.8

Lesson 3

Decimal Addition Word Problems

Solve the problems below.

1. Jeremy is a great basketball player. In season one he averaged 9.3 points with 6.2 rebounds per game. In season two he averaged 24.9 points and 3.6 rebounds per game. In season three he averaged 41.2 points with 6.4 rebounds per game. What was the total of his points and rebound averages for all three seasons?

2. Randy eats way too much ice cream. He ate 1.5 ounces on Monday, 2.3 ounces on Tuesday and 3.6 ounces on Wednesday. Thursday he ate 6.9 ounces . Then on Friday he ate 4.2 ounces of ice cream. How much ice cream did Randy eat in total this week?

3. Cynthia has a parrot named Hank. Hank gets his exercise everyday by flying. On Monday he flew 5.1 miles. On Tuesday he flew 6.85 miles. On Wednesday he flew 2.97 miles. Then on Thursday he flew 4.63 miles. How many miles has Hank flown this week?

4. Dad went fishing today. The first fish he caught weighed 12.39 pounds. The second fish he caught weighed 16.05 pounds. The third fish he caught weighed 2.76 pounds. Finally the last fish he caught weighed 9.14 pounds. What is the total weight of all the fish Dad caught today?

Lesson 4

Adding Decimals 1

Find the totals below.

1.	2.	3.	4.
123.47 34.10 + 8.36	106.05 23.21 + 1.36	253.75 73.36 + 10.15	387.12 49.70 + 6.65

5.	6.	7.	8.
513.08 309.12 + 76.59	480.21 759.96 + 88.07	624.71 267.35 + 20.99	945.37 651.83 + 79.41

9.	10.	11.	12.
11.892 20.624 57.393 + 8.102	.937 13.419 23.757 + 9.144	12.587 6.794 90.725 + 24.431	67.599 11.180 9.413 + 21.924

13.	14.	15.	16.
22.408 641.119 36.327 + 52.176	18.649 97.321 531.655 + 944.299	782.113 430.627 67.511 + 12.549	72.399 194.912 381.134 + 26.709

17.	18.	19.	20.
11.852 224.379 3.991 + 921.104	127.537 363.224 40.916 + 598.644	673.112 260.657 167.320 + 6.279	587.611 76.435 539.907 + 322.621

Adding Decimals 2

Find the totals below.

1.	2.	3.	4.
651.207	300. 498	499.499	549.339
892.890	53. 115	644.466	276.521
509.001	88. 304	320.072	155.277
37.500	216. 224	122.321	608.658
+ 201.605	+ 366. 367	+ 783.009	+ .151

5.	6.	7.	8.
59.650	422.231	500.658	684.942
324.822	7.807	606.822	29.312
715.155	725.237	832.615	654.697
2.777	320.364	299.934	277.347
+ 500.000	+ 967.957	+ 1.307	+ 306.754

9.	10.	11.	12.
5.001	575.575	229.242	930.854
470.120	53.347	301.507	292.304
52.233	699.024	8.111	152.995
375.032	752.990	358.999	904.654
+ 960.197	+ 247.367	+ 295.031	+ 35.002

13.	14.	15.	16.
651.133	865.656	966.865	558.715
326.369	347.211	303.975	669.559
959.900	122.169	288.361	781.375
360.452	607.307	465.205	324.278
+ 995.521	+ 744.654	+ 217.000	+ 587.662

Adding Decimals 3

Find the totals below.

1. 2,418.09 4,334.49 712.64 +1,482.11	**2.** 6,967.24 34.13 5,110.37 +2,326.22	**3.** 2,126.94 3,615.03 24.77 +4,331.62	**4.** 7,269.81 1,382.43 409.30 + 3.99
5. 604.88 7,291.39 3,036.13 +9,123.24	**6.** 4,168.68 5,055.33 4,333.07 + 659.37	**7.** 9,224.54 75.31 4.52 +3,012.10	**8.** 482.00 3,312.67 4,999.60 + 20.54
9. 6,287.90 961.24 823.36 +2,682.48	**10.** 329.58 3,677.41 9,003.36 + 51.27	**11.** 7,622.31 301.02 440.68 +2,539.88	**12.** 5,880.99 5,951.50 47.66 + 9.72
13. 4,408.12 8,399.99 254.17 2,765.55 +7,321.01	**14.** 88.78 9,100.59 65.34 3,036.66 + 7.92	**15.** 1,448.39 6,691.15 2,308.54 279.02 + 35.37	**16.** 5,651.14 9,842.59 2,000.77 2,621.22 +2,903.00

Lesson 5

Decimal Points Subtraction

Subtracting decimals is like normal subtraction.
You just have to remember to line up the decimals.

Hint: Decimal points always go at the end of a whole number (6 = 6.0 or 6.00)

Example: Subtract 20.99 from 44.5

Step 1: Line up the decimals.	**Step 2:** Add zeros and borrow when needed.	**Step 3:** Subtract all the numbers.
	3 14	3 14
44.5	4~~4~~.~~5~~[1]0	4~~4~~.~~5~~[1]0
– 20.99	– 20.99	– 20.99
		23.51

Line up the decimals and solve the problems below.
Show your work in the boxes.

1. 9.25 - 4.7

```
  9.25
- 4.70
------
  4.55
```

2. 30.5 - 17.05

3. 28.12 - .72

4. 605 - 45.07

5. 94.99 - 6.34

6. 339 - 40.09

Lesson 6

Arranging and Subtracting Decimals 1

Subtracting decimals is like normal subtraction.
You just have to remember to line up the decimals.

Hint: Decimal points always go at the end of a whole number (6 = 6.0 or 6.00)

Line up the decimals and solve the problems below.

1. 72.53 - 22.56

2. 99.58 - 71.90

3. 33.29 - 19.4

4. 40.06 - 24.1

5. 59.19 - 58.02

6. 82.33 - 51.73

7. 29.23 - 11.06

8. 95.19 - 48.44

9. 80 .46 - 62.9

Arranging and Subtracting Decimals 2

Subtracting decimals is like normal subtraction.
You just have to remember to line up the decimals.

Hint: Decimal points always go at the end of a whole number (6 = 6.0 or 6.00)

Line up the decimals and solve the problems below.

1. 695.53 - 103.08

2. 851.12 - 48.90

3. 305.94 - 12.44

4. 437.2 - 399.56

5. 229.16 - 116.95

6. 821.63 - 354.7

7. 537.21 - 37.59

8. 302.99 - 199.05

9. 900.56 - 621.07

Arranging and Subtracting Decimals 3

Subtracting decimals is like normal subtraction.
You just have to remember to line up the decimals.

Hint: Decimal points always go at the end of a whole number (6 = 6.0 or 6.00)

Line up the decimals and solve the problems below.

1. 81.953 - 2.641

2. 39.058 - 2.806

3. 66.491 - 11.08

4. 68.094 - 7.687

5. 22.916 - 11.695

6. 339.1 - .799

7. 53.210 - 37.059

8. 14 - 7.095

9. 579.802 - .07

Lesson 7

Subtracting Decimals 1

Subtract the amounts below.

1. 231.57 − 182.24	**2.** 432.66 − 106.27	**3.** 379.20 − 273.94	**4.** 628.12 − 504.39
5. 611.32 − 369.48	**6.** 461.30 − 119.82	**7.** 654.55 − 307.47	**8.** 859.00 − 689.38
9. 741.99 − 207.64	**10.** 584.37 − 119.01	**11.** 615.06 − 527.92	**12.** 363.19 − 329.75
13. 64.982 − 20.191	**14.** 32.100 − 12.086	**15.** 52.604 − 39.335	**16.** 11.325 − 5.425
17. 67.385 − 46.105	**18.** 90.488 − 53.914	**19.** 75.672 − 33.127	**20.** 36.854 − 11.367

Subtracting Decimals 2

Subtract the amounts below.

1. 1,334.62 − 451.39	**2.** 2,485.12 − 384.67	**3.** 4,645.14 − 185.33	**4.** 3,313.74 − 599.91
5. 5,482.49 − 420.24	**6.** 7,893.72 − 599.32	**7.** 6,820.47 − 875.97	**8.** 2,339.00 − 922.11
9. 5,894.27 −3,554.72	**10.** 8,775.54 −3,997.32	**11.** 7,654.41 −5,229.80	**12.** 9,501.64 −8,329.33
13. 628.399 −175.508	**14.** 977.687 −345.113	**15.** 710.910 − 84.456	**16.** 527.842 −211.611
17. 139.209 − 44.364	**18.** 374.346 −171.712	**19.** 452.833 −299.425	**20.** 926.001 −364.967

Subtracting Decimals 3

Subtract the amounts below.

1. 49.9262 − 32.6139	**2.** 69.8420 − 29.9609	**3.** 39.7124 − 18.2570	**4.** 84.4962 − 38.8691
5. 720.581 − 556.512	**6.** 521.003 − 352.109	**7.** 120.589 − 100.075	**8.** 264.892 − 155.684
9. 49,078.2 −38,865.1	**10.** 8,009.01 −6,420.57	**11.** 9,569.25 −3,365.72	**12.** 7.65940 − 2.29995
13. 3,965.21 −1,788.95	**14.** 548.722 − 345.871	**15.** 2.99265 − .95846	**16.** 90.0364 − 77.8205
17. 89,756.1 −15,672.7	**18.** 77,582.1 −56,963.8	**19.** 33,587.2 −19,985.7	**20.** 9,987.02 −8,908.25

Lesson 8

Decimal Subtraction Word Problems

Solve the problems below.

1. Mike needs to swim 6 miles a week to get strong enough to make the swim team. On Monday he swam 1.34 miles. On Tuesday he swam 2.49 miles. On Wednesday he swam .82 miles. How much further must he swim to reach his goal of 6 miles?

2. Jenny wants to lift 100 pounds of weight each day. First she lifted 10.57 pounds, then she lifted 29.96 pounds. Next she lifted 32.65 pounds. How much more weight does she need to lift to reach her goal ?

3. Newt needs a total of 300 points on his school projects to go on the field trip. On the first project he scored 86.57 points. On the second project he scored 95.36 points. On the next project he scored 64.11 points. How many more points must he score to go on the trip?

4. James was using so much water playing in the sprinkler that his mom set a limit of 15 gallons per week. On the first day he used 2.65 gallons. On the second day he used 3.21 gallons. On the third day James used 4.81 gallons. Then on the fourth day he used 1.92 gallons. How much water does James have left this week?

Lesson 9

Adding Money 1

The rules that we learned for adding decimals is also how we add money.

289.64		\$289.64
+ 56.11	=	+ \$56.11
345.75		\$345.75

Find the totals below.

1.	2.	3.	4.
\$103.32	\$315.15	\$91.64	\$144.75
+ \$49.08	+ \$12.99	+ \$296.12	+ \$82.32
\$152.40			

5.	6.	7.	8.
\$257.95	\$642.44	\$309.37	\$914.70
+ \$189.05	+ \$791.17	+ \$276.24	+ \$367.05

9.	10.	11.	12.
\$454.12	\$708.51	\$34.33	\$691.11
\$59.99	\$623.78	\$551.40	\$320.95
+ \$375.36	+ \$11.63	+ \$186.17	+ \$64.32

13.	14.	15.	16.
\$111.88	\$399.23	\$607.14	\$119.67
\$965.42	\$499.67	\$324.24	\$394.66
+ \$375.30	+ \$233.99	+ \$178.17	+ \$367.92

Adding Money 2

Find the totals below.

1.	2.	3.	4.
$108.22	$56.44	$480.55	$365.99
$399.08	$275.17	$59.63	$264.56
+ $12.28	+ $2.36	+ $237.11	+ $12.00

5.	6.	7.	8.
$564.23	$216.21	$754.55	$908.09
$257.67	$347.96	$191.19	$124.64
+ $106.63	+ $964.07	+ $267.67	+ $573.11

9.	10.	11.	12.
$245.77	$210.11	$662.95	$302.34
$331.06	$772.72	$97.84	$475.62
$24.33	$186.80	$205.04	$65.24
+ $100.97	+ $67.29	+ $177.00	+ $134.89

13.	14.	15.	16.
$905.15	$488.88	$625.33	$723.99
$465.55	$706.11	$233.31	$949.12
$992.61	$300.37	$914.45	$811.34
+ $133.21	+ $511.77	+ $928.17	+ $267.09

17.	18.	19.	20.
$635.01	$500.49	$368.84	$299.02
$199.11	$1.11	$675.64	$103.65
$208.28	$600.59	$99.30	$690.31
+ $322.37	+ $37.64	+ $261.71	+ $782.57

Lesson 10

Subtracting Money 1

Now that you know how to subtract decimals, use what you've learned to answer these money problems.

15.63		\$15.63
- 2.12	=	- \$2.12
13.51		\$13.51

Subtract the amounts below.

1. \$6.22 - \$3.84 = \$2.38	**2.** \$4.70 - \$1.35	**3.** \$3.84 - \$1.99	**4.** \$7.79 - \$5.32
5. \$8.84 - \$3.53	**6.** \$6.85 - \$5.06	**7.** \$9.98 - \$6.16	**8.** \$9.27 - \$4.64
9. \$8.99 - \$6.13	**10.** \$3.08 - \$.94	**11.** \$7.12 - \$5.37	**12.** \$6.39 - \$2.17
13. \$135.07 - \$75.98	**14.** \$209.47 - \$105.12	**15.** \$466.17 - \$389.55	**16.** \$349.68 - \$127.35
17. \$859.07 - \$407.98	**18.** \$654.00 - \$332.37	**19.** \$567.25 - \$125.74	**20.** \$804.91 - \$722.05

Subtracting Money 2

Subtract the amounts below.

1. $275.29 − $107.72

2. $535.11 − $299.39

3. $332.88 − $111.49

4. $630.00 − $424.84

5. $643.17 − $307.51

6. $800.99 − $115.35

7. $772.63 − $631.51

8. $704.90 − $639.17

9. $551.12 − $337.94

10. $675.99 − $167.91

11. $240.11 − $177.54

12. $999.00 − $327.29

13. $490.17 − $215.05

14. $807.00 − $318.37

15. $420.34 − $385.94

16. $788.40 − $264.19

17. $711.72 − $499.07

18. $470.97 − $295.48

19. $849.84 − $601.31

20. $511.31 − $294.52

Lesson 11

Decimal Points Multiplication

To multiply decimals, start by multiplying the numbers just as if they were whole numbers.

Example: Multiply 4.22 by 3.5

Step 1:	Step 2:	Step 3:
Line up the numbers on the right - **do not align the decimal points.**	Starting on the right, multiply each digit in the top number by each digit in the bottom number, just as with whole numbers. Then add the products.	Place the decimal point in the answer by starting at the right and moving the number of places equal to the sum of the decimal places in both numbers multiplied.
4.22 x 3.5	4.22 x 3.5 2110 +12660 14770	4.22 ← 2 decimal places + x 3.5 ← 1 decimal place 2110 +12660 14.770 ← 3 decimal places

Multiply the problems below and correctly align the decimals.

1. 8.3 x 6.4 332 +4980 53.12	**2.** 3.3 x 2.9	**3.** 6.7 x 4.4	**4.** 5.9 x 3.6	**5.** 4.5 x 2.9
6. 8.5 x 6.7	**7.** 4.9 x 2.7	**8.** 9.8 x 6.2	**9.** 7.7 x 5.8	**10.** 9.5 x 8.2
11. 8.8 x 7.4	**12.** 5.9 x 5.7	**13.** 6.2 x 4.9	**14.** 4.3 x 2.5	**15.** 8.7 x 3.9

Lesson 12

Multiplying Decimals 1

Multiply the problems below and correctly align the decimals.

1. 4.2 9 x 5.3 2 2.7 3 7	**2.** 6.8 5 x .8 6	**3.** 3.4 2 x 1.3	**4.** 5.3 7 x 6.4	**5.** 7.3 2 x 2.6
6. 8 5.5 x .3 2	**7.** 6 3.1 x .5 6	**8.** 2 9.4 x 4 9	**9.** 9.9 9 x .8 3	**10.** 6 7.2 x 2.9
11. .2 4 9 x .9 7	**12.** 4 3.3 x 2 3	**13.** 5 5.3 x .5 8	**14.** 6 8.2 x 4.3	**15.** .9 2 7 x 7.2
16. 7 7.3 x 2.4	**17.** 2.4 5 x .8 4	**18.** 8 2.7 x 2.7	**19.** 5 6.6 x 9 9	**20.** 6.0 8 x . 6 7
21. 8.5 2 x 3.7	**22.** 5 9.9 x 6.6	**23.** 2.8 7 x 9.4	**24.** 3 6.2 x .5 5	**25.** 9.0 4 x 4 9

Multiplying Decimals 2

Multiply the problems below and correctly align the decimals.

1. 18.32 x 6.8	**2.** 44.09 x .33	**3.** 22.39 x 74	**4.** 57.82 x 2.9	**5.** 77.32 x .55
6. 3.447 x 4.1	**7.** 5.772 x 59	**8.** 33.47 x 3.3	**9.** 662.5 x 1.4	**10.** 4.262 x 5.7
11. 8299 x .88	**12.** 429.8 x 4.1	**13.** 5.723 x 63	**14.** 864.1 x .59	**15.** 93.22 x 2.9
16. 7.085 x 37	**17.** 367.5 x 4.5	**18.** 94.47 x .83	**19.** 7.245 x 7.6	**20.** 32.64 x 5.9
21. 995.3 x 8.4	**22.** 8127 x .99	**23.** 5.333 x 6.6	**24.** 81.24 x .34	**25.** 96.77 x 7.7

Multiplying Decimals 3

Multiply the problems below and correctly align the decimals.

1. 239.4 x 3.92	**2.** 7.863 x 45.5	**3.** 53.22 x 8.45	**4.** 4.977 x .368	**5.** 369.9 x 15.4
6. 23.18 x 53.6	**7.** 946.2 x .337	**8.** 4.556 x 66.8	**9.** 327.4 x 4.19	**10.** 5.585 x 72.5
11. .7269 x 342	**12.** 465.7 x 59.9	**13.** 3.697 x 23.5	**14.** 22.42 x 8.29	**15.** 6.823 x 37.7
16. 593.7 x 92.5	**17.** 7.557 x 82.7	**18.** 952.9 x 6.34	**19.** 3.669 x 29.2	**20.** 5247 x 7.94

Chapter 6 - Geometry

Chapter 6 - Geometry

In this chapter you will learn about shapes and geometry. **Here is what you will learn:**

- Identifying Flat Shapes
- Polygons
- Finding Area of Shapes
- Finding Perimeter
- Identifying Solid Shapes
- Understanding Circles

  (Radius, Diameter, Circumference)
- Understanding Points, Lines and Rays
- Understanding Angles
- Understanding Volume

Flat Shapes

Shapes can come in any size and can have many sides. Here are the flat shapes you will learn about in this chapter.
Circle
(1 side)
Triangle
(3 sides)
Rectangle
(4 sides)
Square
(4 sides)
Rhombus
(4 sides)
Parallelogram
(4 sides)
Trapezoid
(4 sides)
Pentagon
(5 sides)
Hexagon
(6 sides)
Heptagon
(7 sides)
Octagon
(8 sides)
Nonagon
(9 sides)
Decagon
(10 sides)

Lesson 1

Understanding Polygons

- A **polygon** is a closed plane figure made up of 3 or more line segments.
- Polygons that have all sides of equal length are called regular polygons.
- Polygons are named depending on the number of lines that form their boundaries.

Here are some examples of **polygons**:

Triangle:
A polygon with three sides

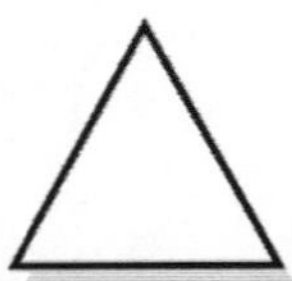

Quadrilateral
A polygon with four sides.

Pentagon
A polygon with five sides

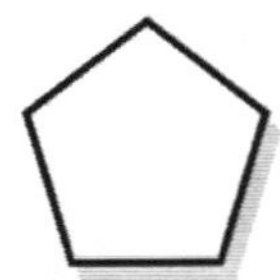

A **quadrilateral** is a four-sided polygon. Here are some types of **quadrilateral** shapes:

Rectangle: A parallelogram with four right angles.

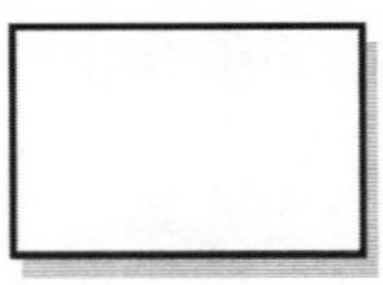

Square: A parallelogram with four congruent sides and four right angles.

Trapezoid: A quadrilateral with only one pair of parallel sides.

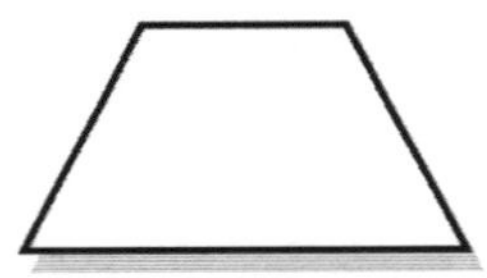

Parallelogram: A quadrilateral with two pairs of opposite sides parallel.

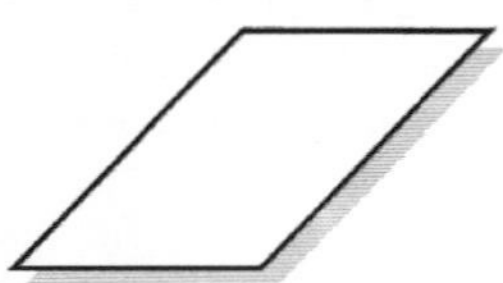

Rhombus: A parallelogram with four congruent sides.

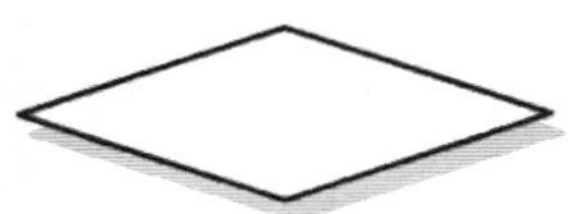

Lesson 2

Finding Area of Squares and Rectangles

Area is the measurement of a shape's surface area.
To find the **area** of a square, multiply the length by the width.

109 ft.

44 ft.

Area = 109 ft. x 44 ft. = 4,796 $ft.^2$

Area = 4,796 $ft.^2$

Find the area of each shape. Write the problem out.

1. 74 in.

74 in.

74in. x 74in. = 5,476 $in.^2$

2. 134 ft.

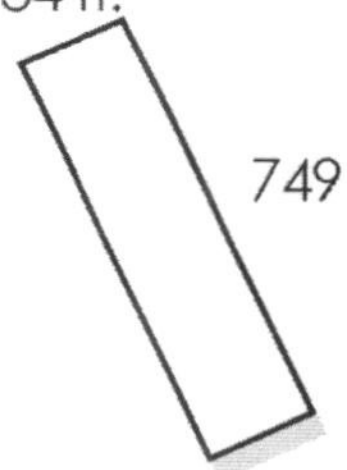

749 ft.

3.

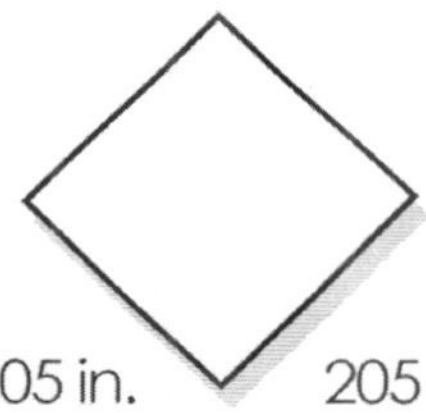

205 in. 205 in.

4. 299 ft.

436 ft.

5. 637 in.

637 in.

6. 1,262 yd.

507 yd.

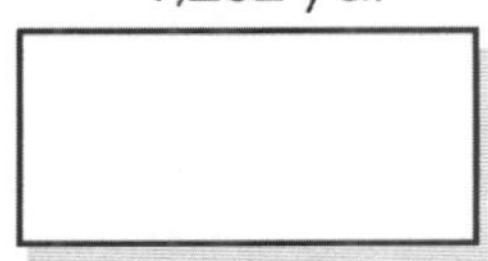

Lesson 3

Finding Area of Triangles

To find the **area** of a **triangle** use the formula below:

Area = $\frac{1}{2}$ of base x height

Area = 14in. x 8in. ÷ 2 = 56 in.^{2}

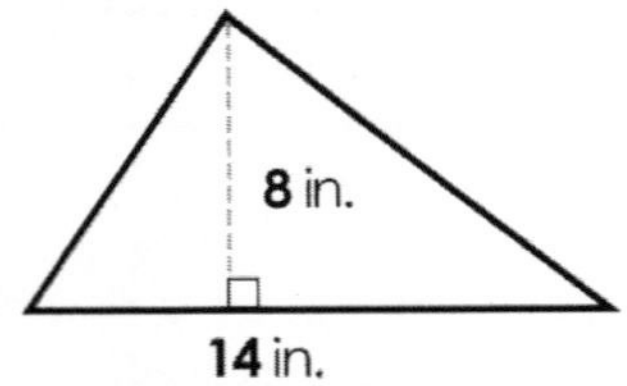

Find the area of each triangle. Write the problem out.

1.
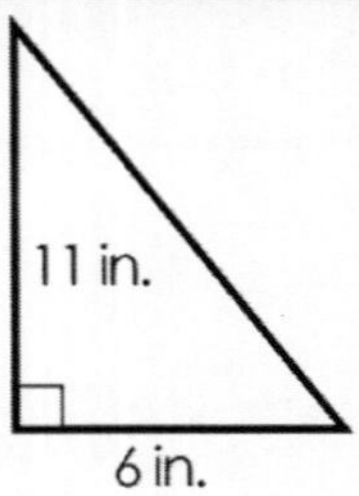

11in. x 6in. ÷ 2 = 33 in.^{2}

2.
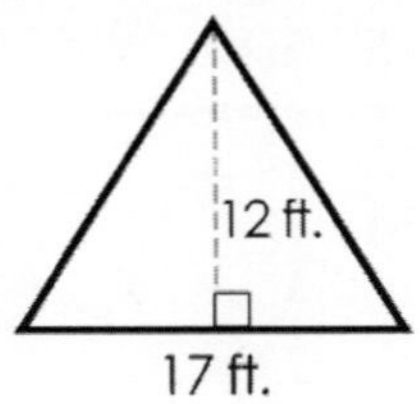

____

3.
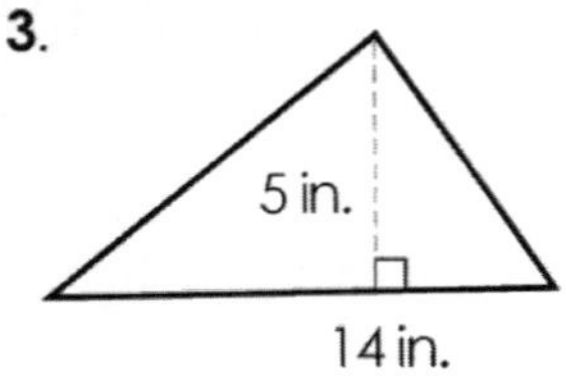

____

4.
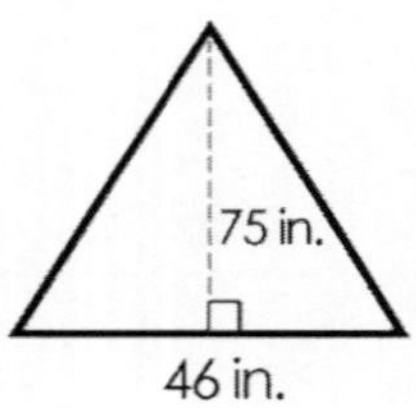

____

5.
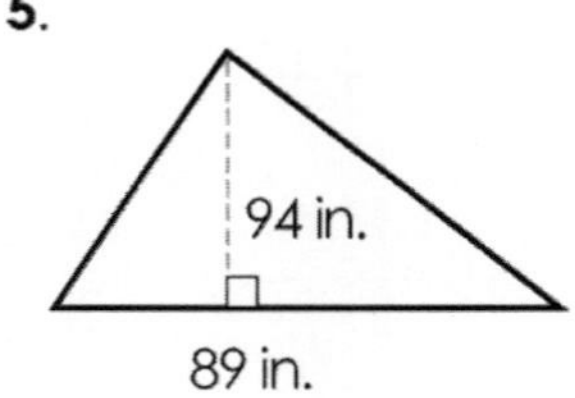

____

6.
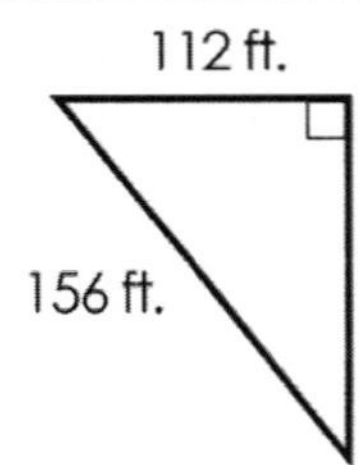

____

Lesson 4

Finding Area of Parallelograms

To find the area of a parallelogram use what we learned before and multiply height times width.

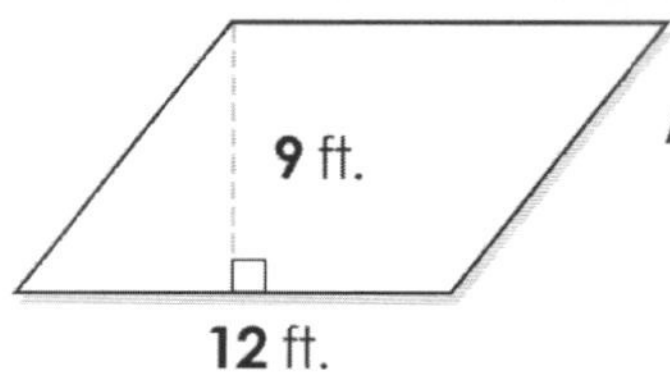

Area = 12 ft. x 9 ft. = 108 ft.^{2}

Area = 108 ft.^{2}

Find the area of each parallelogram. Write the problem out.

1.

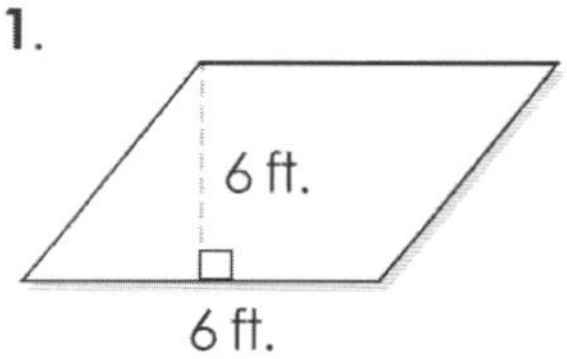

6 ft. x 6 ft. = 36 ft.^{2}

2.

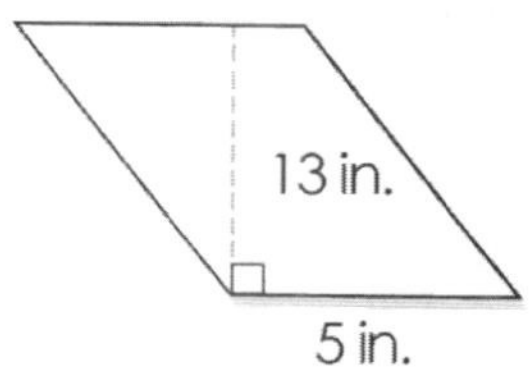

____

3.

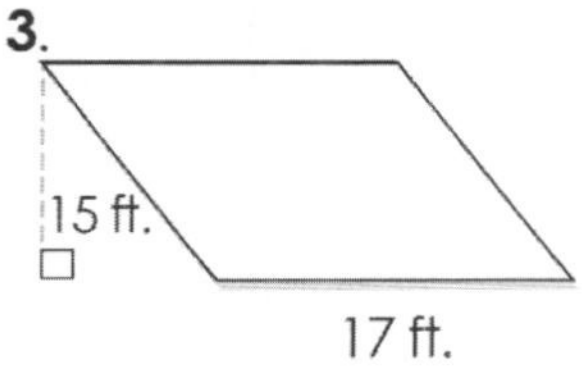

____

4.

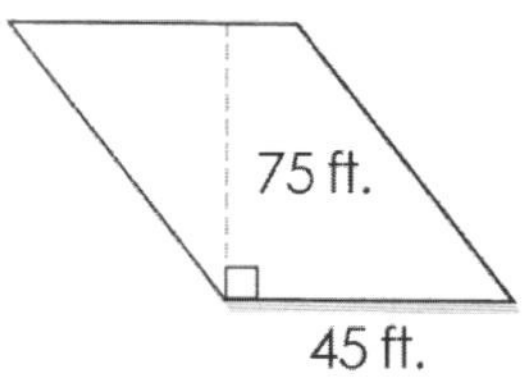

____

5.

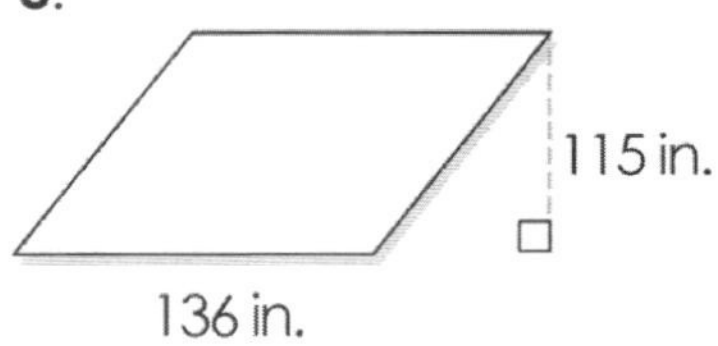

____

6.

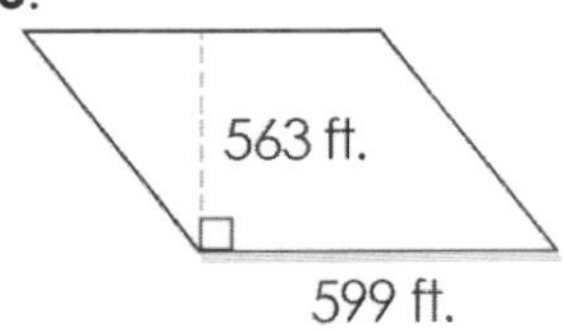

____

Lesson 5

Finding Area of Trapezoids

To find the **area** of a **trapezoid** use this formula:

Area = $\frac{1}{2}$ of (base 1 + base 2 x height)

Step 1: Add the bases. 5 + 14 = 19	**Step 2:** Multiply base totals by height. 19 x 8 = 152	**Step 3:** Divide that total by 2. 152 ÷ 2 = 76
Area = 5 + 14 x 8 ÷ 2 = 76		

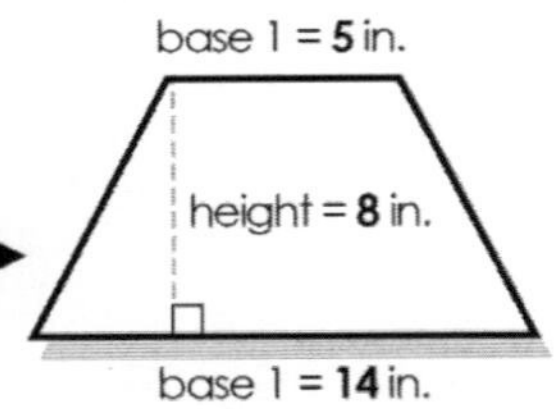

Area = 76 in.^{2}

Find the area of each trapezoid. Write the problem out.

1.

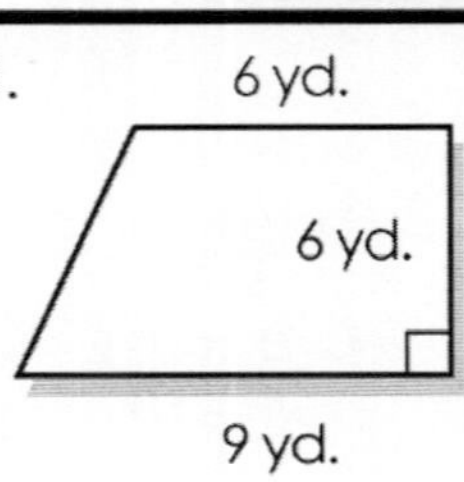

6 + 9 x 6 ÷ 2 = 45 yd.^{2}

2.

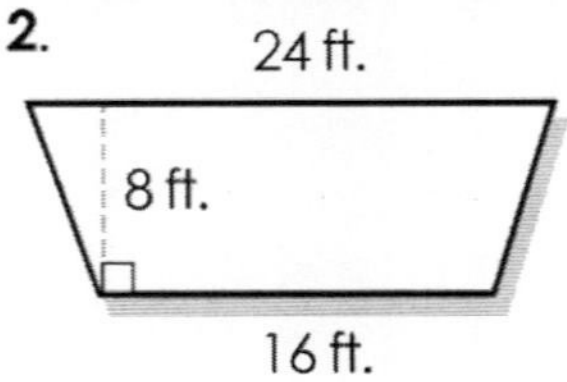

____

3.

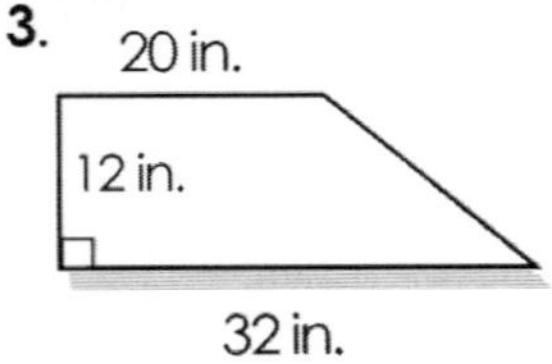

____

4.

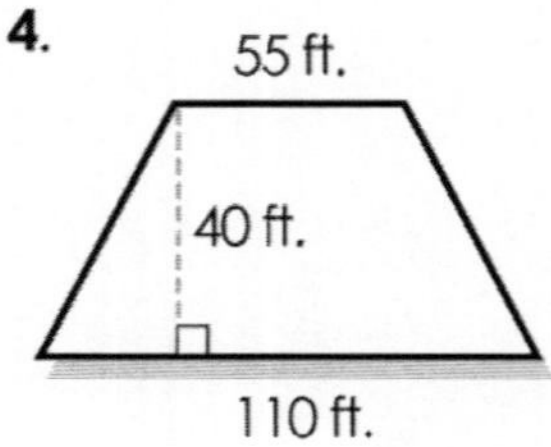

____

5.

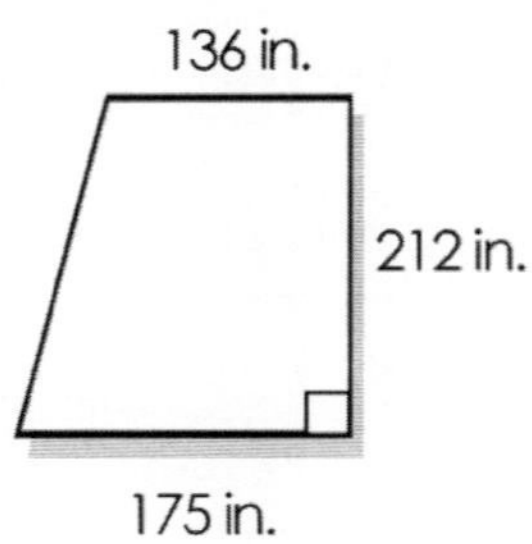

____

6.

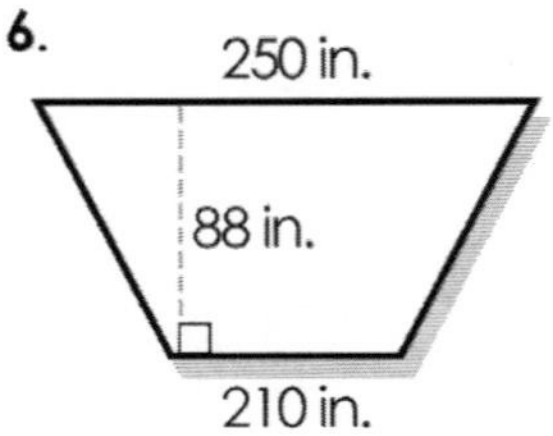

____

Lesson 6

Finding Perimeter 1

Perimeter is the distance around an object.
Find the perimeter of each object by adding all the sides.

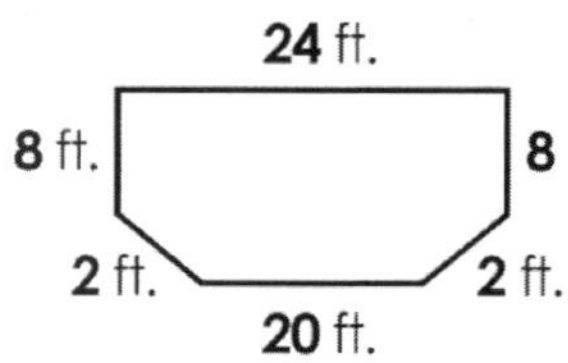

Perimeter = 24 ft. + 20 ft. + 8 ft. + 8 ft. + 2 ft. + 2 ft.

Perimeter = 64 ft.

Find the perimeter of each shape. Write the problem out.

1.

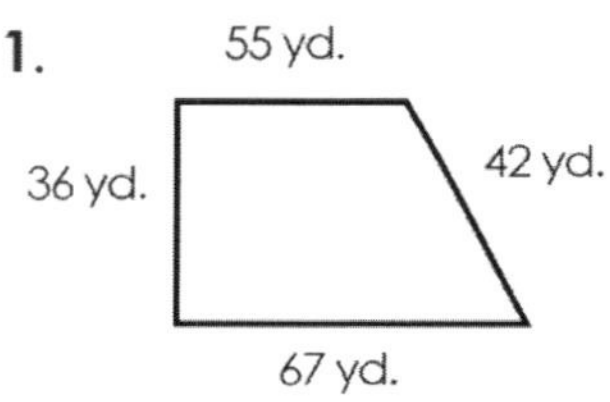

36 + 67 + 55 + 42 = 197 yd.

2.

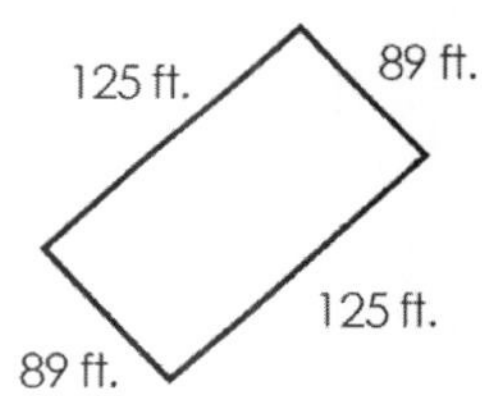

____

3.

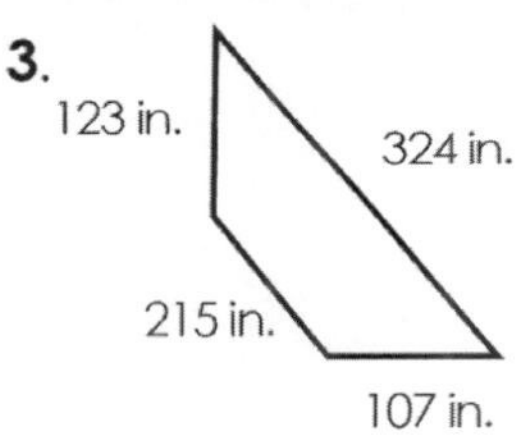

____

4.

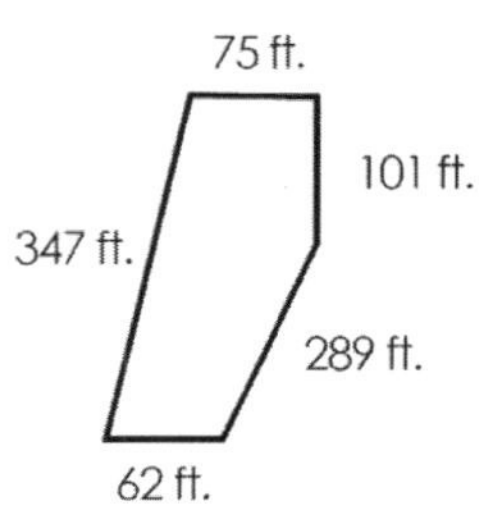

____

5.

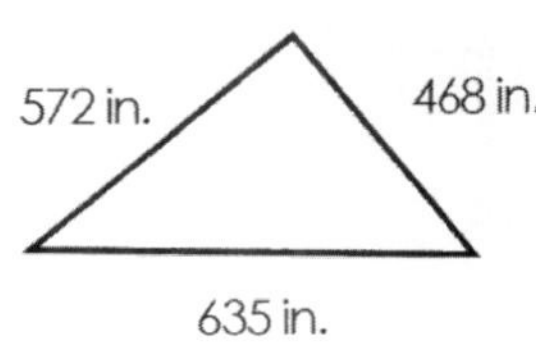

____

6.

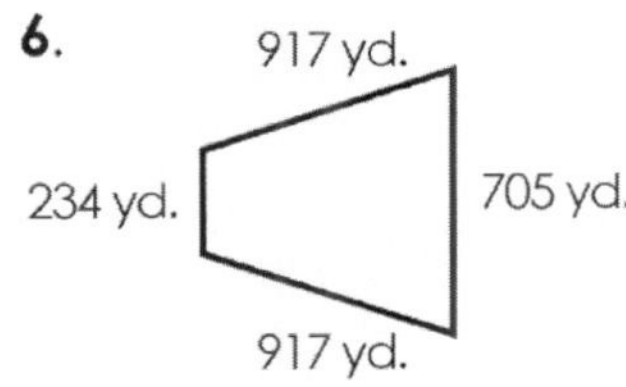

____

Finding Perimeter 2

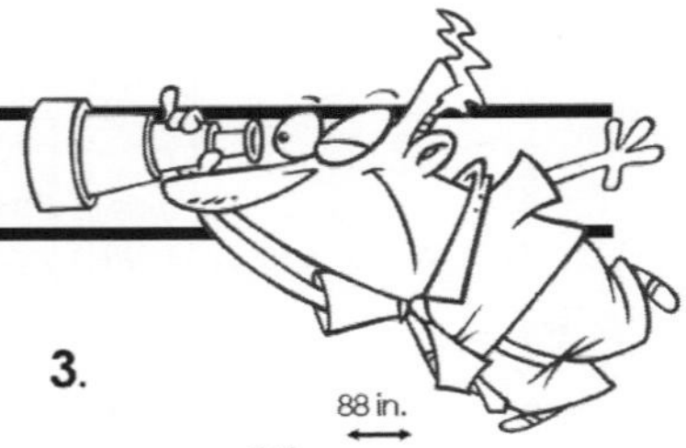

Find the perimeter of each shape. Write the problem out.

1.

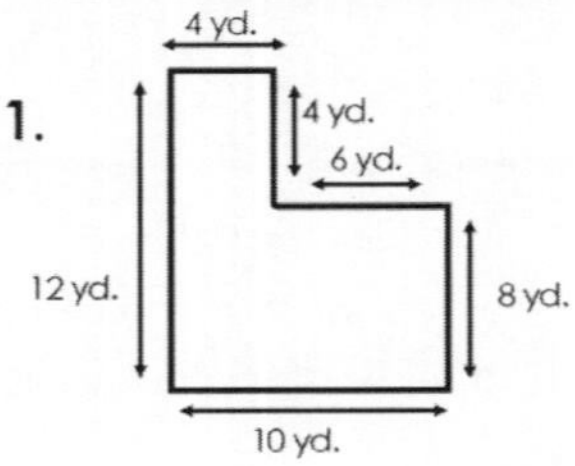

2.

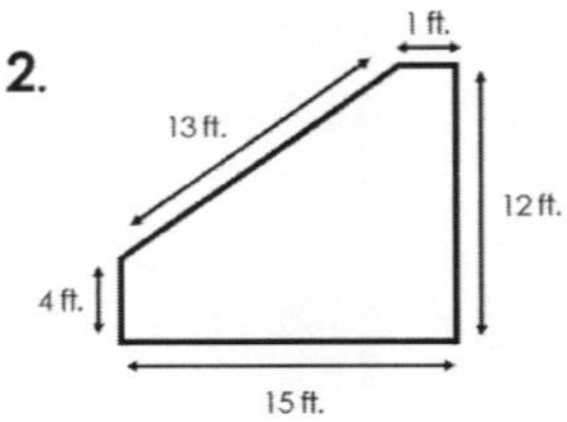

3.

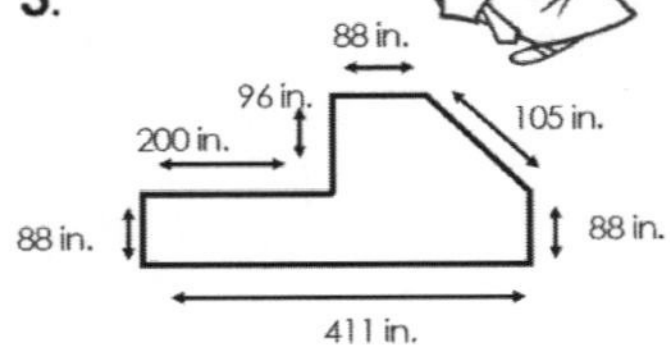

4.

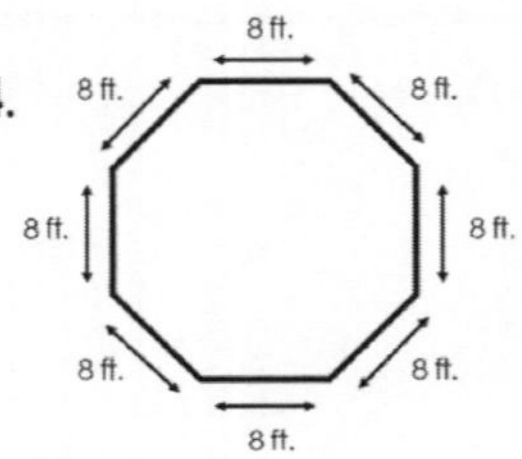

5.

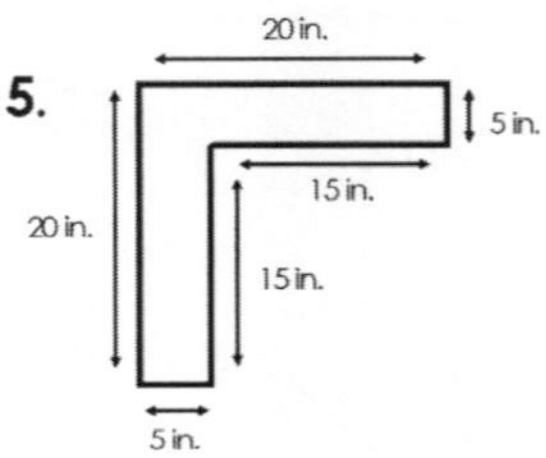

6.

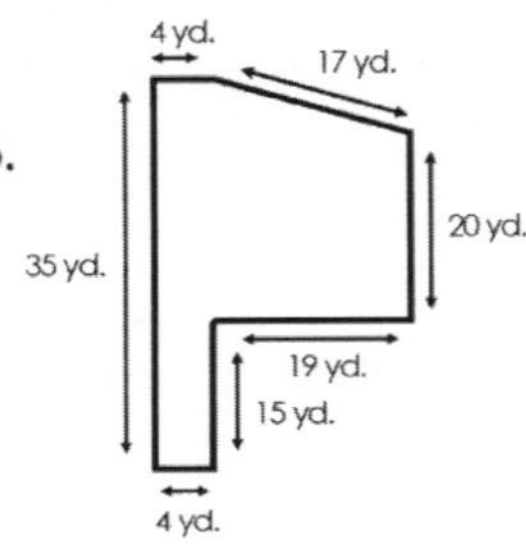

7.

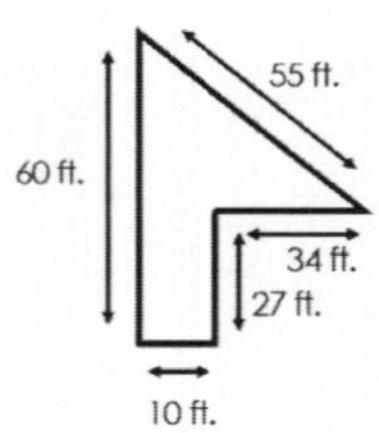

8.

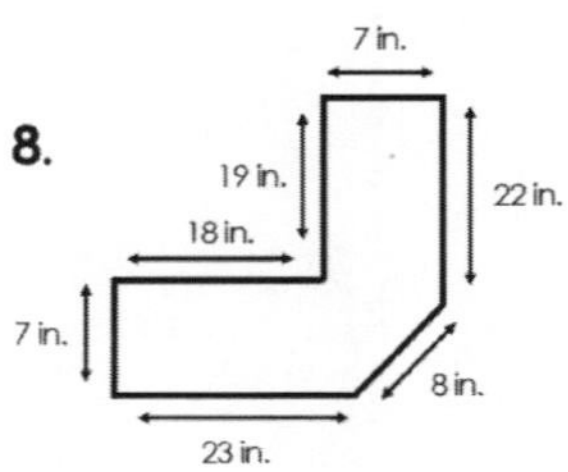

9.

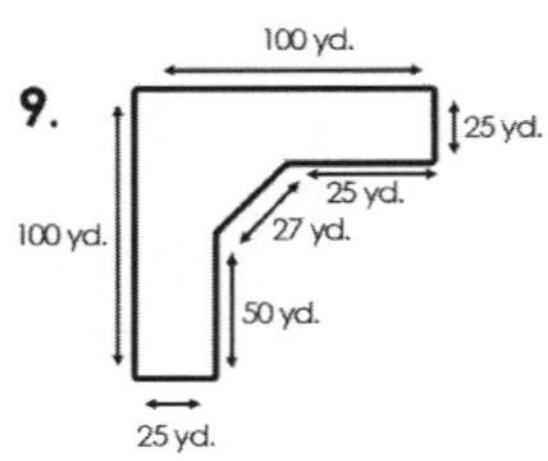

Lesson 7

Identifying Points, Lines and Rays

A **point** is an exact location in space.	A **line** is an endless straight path.	A **line segment** is a straight path between two points.	A **ray** is a part of a line; it has one endpoint and continues on in one direction.	A **vertex** is a point where two or more rays or line segments meet or cross.

Identify and write how many of each set of figures below.

1. 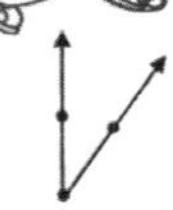

vertex, 1

ray, 2

point, 2

2. 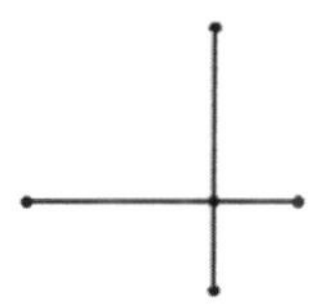

3. 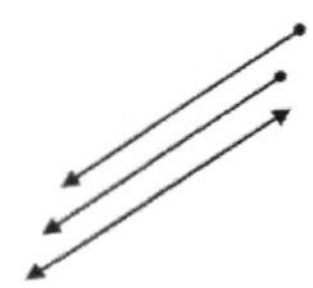

4. 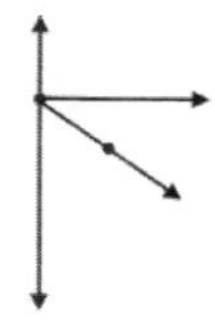

5. 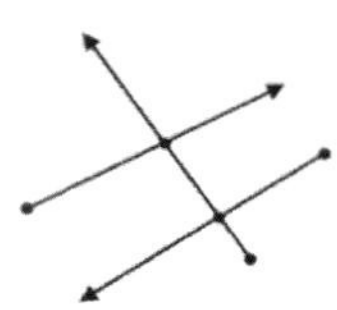

6. 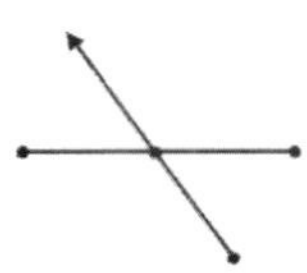

7. 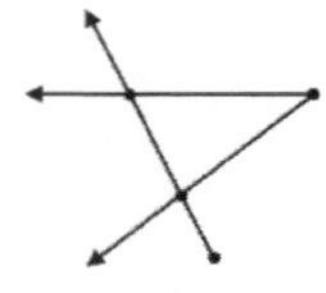

8. 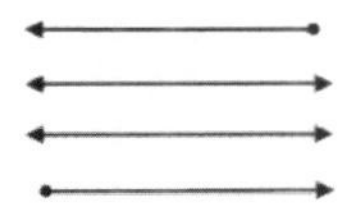

Lesson 8

Identifying Parts of an Angle

- Angles are determined by points and rays.
- This angle is named - ∠ABC.
- This angle is made up of rays AB and CB.
- The vertex of ∠ABC is the point B.

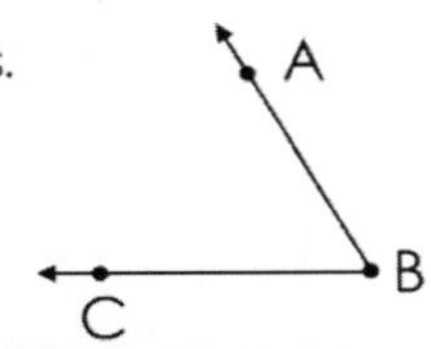

Identify the vertex, rays and names of each angle.

1.

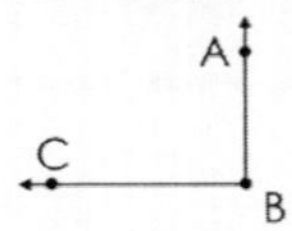

Angle: ABC

Vertex: B

Rays: AB, CB

2.

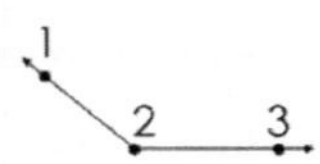

Angle: ________

Vertex: ________

Rays: ________

3.

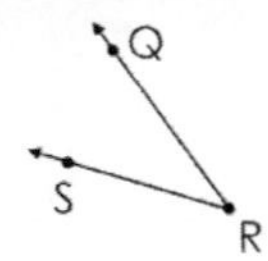

Angle: ________

Vertex: ________

Rays: ________

4.

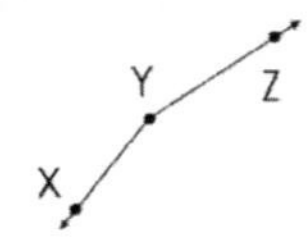

Angle: ________

Vertex: ________

Rays: ________

5.

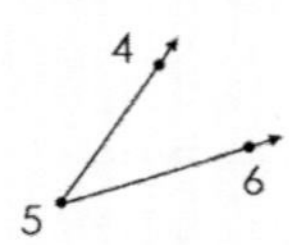

Angle: ________

Vertex: ________

Rays: ________

6.

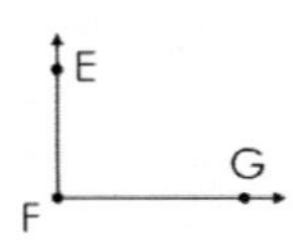

Angle: ________

Vertex: ________

Rays: ________

7.

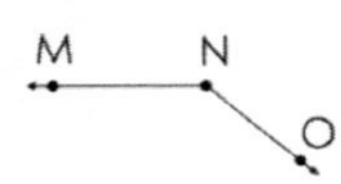

Angle: ________

Vertex: ________

Rays: ________

8.

Angle: ________

Vertex: ________

Rays: ________

9.

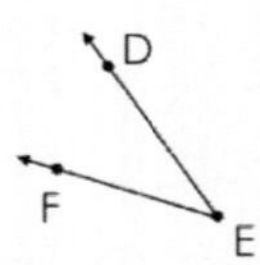

Angle: ________

Vertex: ________

Rays: ________

10.

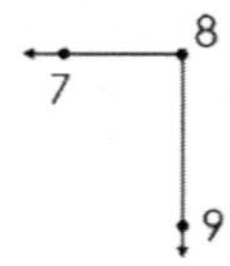

Angle: ________

Vertex: ________

Rays: ________

11.

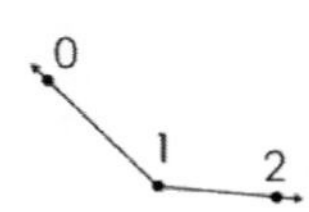

Angle: ________

Vertex: ________

Rays: ________

12.

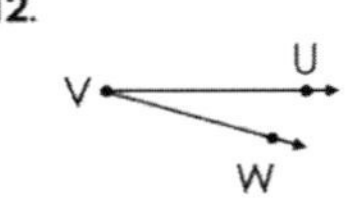

Angle: ________

Vertex: ________

Rays: ________

Solid Shapes

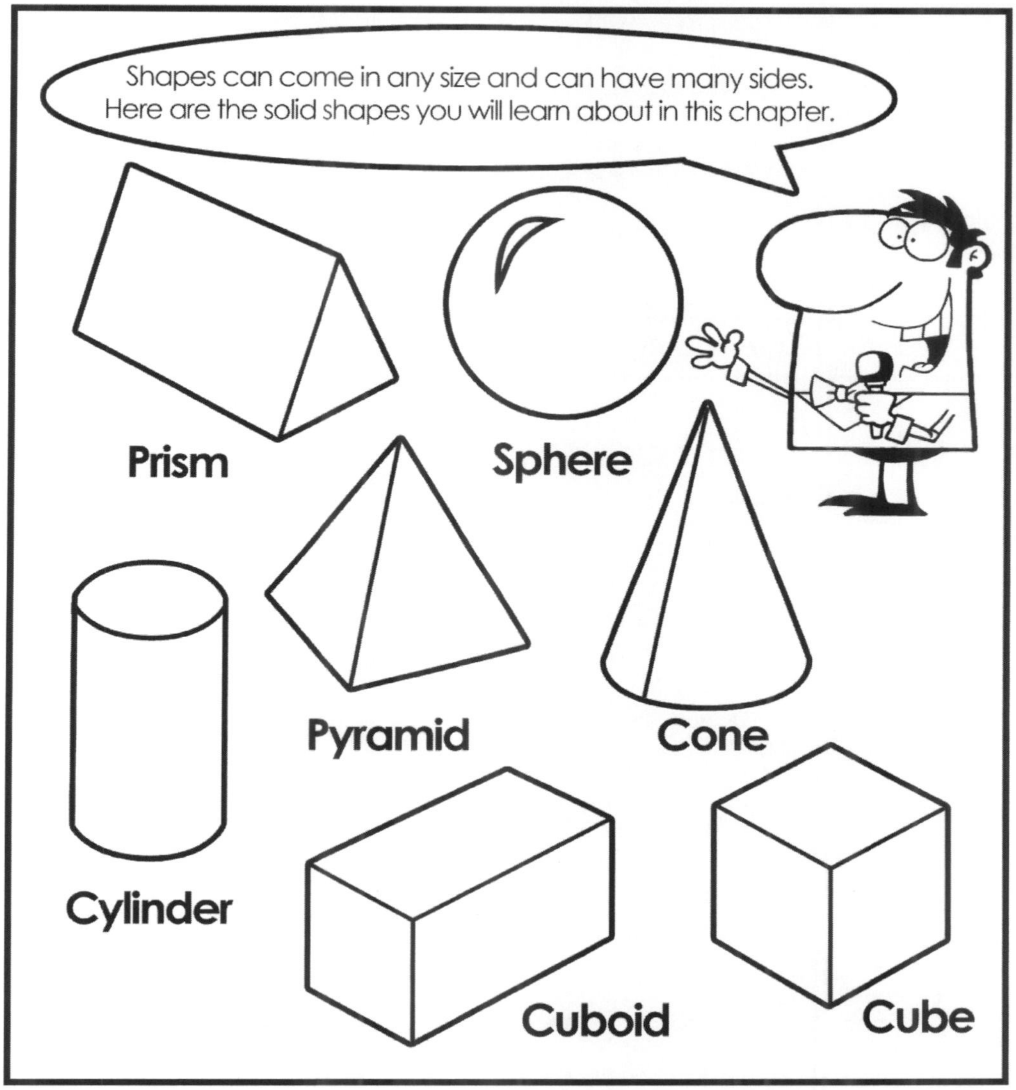

Lesson 9

Identifying Solid Shapes 1

Solid shapes are three-dimensional, non-flat figures. The names of the shapes are determined by the surfaces.

Solid shapes have surfaces, edges and vertices.

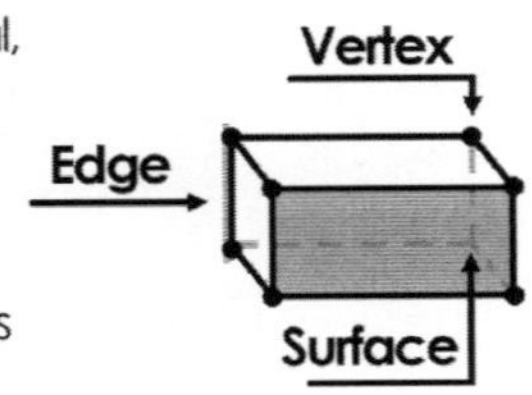

Write the name under each shape and answer the questions below.

1. 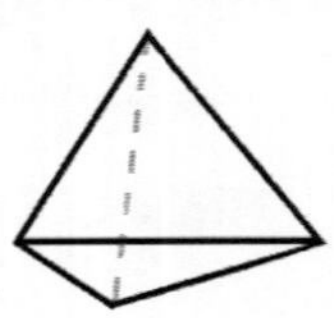

   a. How many **vertices** does this shape have? ________

   b. How many **edges** does this shape have? ________

   c. How many **surfaces** does this shape have? ________

   ____

2. 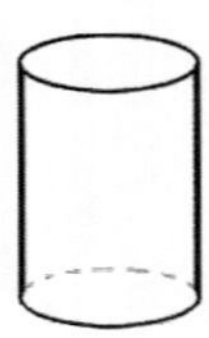

   a. How many **vertices** does this shape have? ________

   b. How many **edges** does this shape have? ________

   c. How many **surfaces** does this shape have? ________

   ____

3. 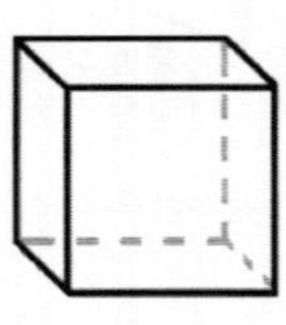

   a. How many **vertices** does this shape have? ________

   b. How many **edges** does this shape have? ________

   c. How many **surfaces** does this shape have? ________

   ____

Identifying Solid Shapes 2

Solid shapes are three-dimensional, non-flat figures. The names of the shapes are determined by the surfaces.

Solid shapes have surfaces, edges and vertices.

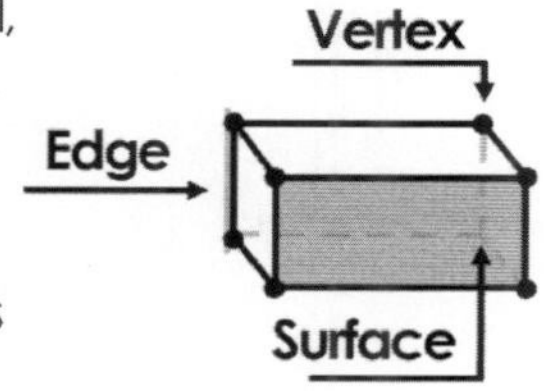

Write the name under each shape and answer the questions below.

1.

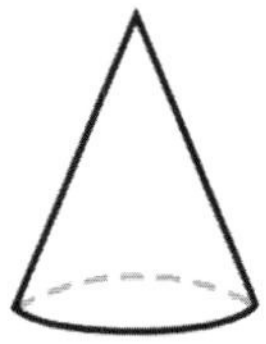

____

a. How many **vertices** does this shape have? ______________

b. How many **edges** does this shape have? ______________

c. How many **surfaces** does this shape have? ______________

2.

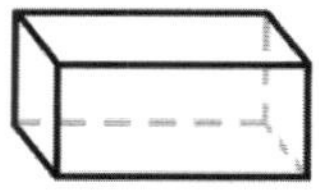

____

a. How many **vertices** does this shape have? ______________

b. How many **edges** does this shape have? ______________

c. How many **surfaces** does this shape have? ______________

3.

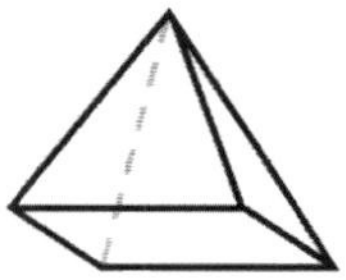

____

a. How many **vertices** does this shape have? ______________

b. How many **edges** does this shape have? ______________

c. How many **surfaces** does this shape have? ______________

Lesson 10

Circles

Now we will learn about the components that make up a circle.
With a circle we have the **radius**, **diameter** and the **circumference**.
Knowing these components will help you to solve problems related to circles.

Radius

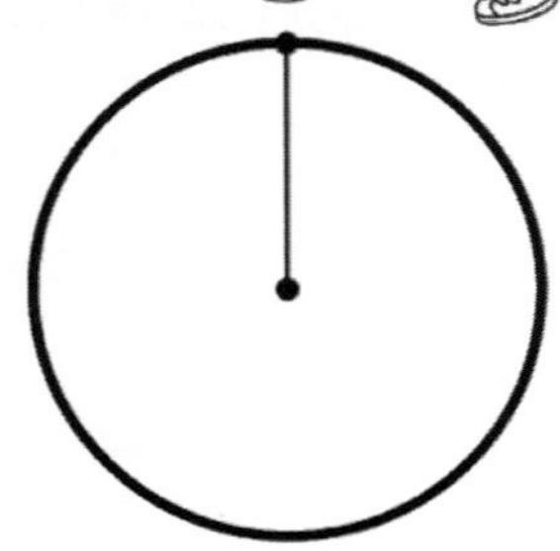

The **radius** of a circle is the distance from the circle's center point to any point on the circle. It can be used to determine a circle's diameter, circumference and area. Because of the circle's shape, the radius can be drawn in anywhere in the center of the circle.

Use this formula to find the radius of a circle:
Radius = Diameter ÷ 2

Diameter

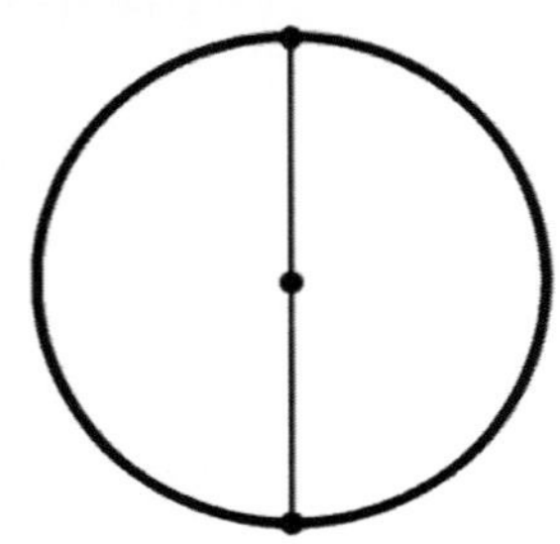

The **diameter** of a circle is the length of a straight line through the center of a circle and touching two points on its edge, the diameter is twice the measurement of the radius. It is the longest distance across the circle. If the diameter of a circle is known, dividing it by two will equal the radius.

Use this formula to find the diameter of a circle:
Diameter = Radius x 2

Circumference

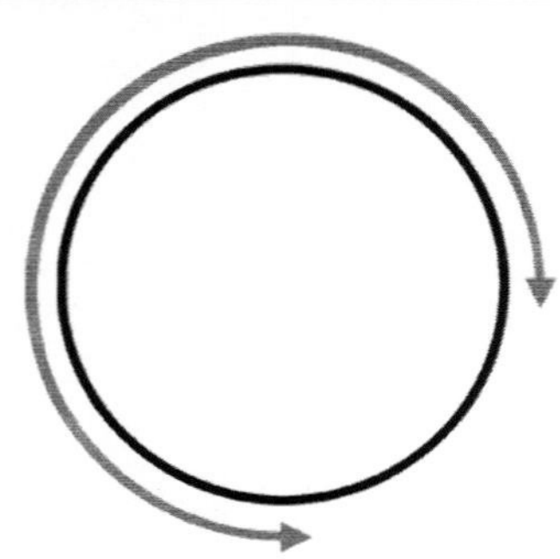

A circle's **circumference** is the distance around the circle. To determine the circumference of a circle, multiply the diameter by pi (π), or multiply the radius by 2 then multiply by pi (π). π is a Greek letter used in math to represent 3.14.

Use this formula to find the diameter of a circle:
Circumference = π x diameter or π x radius x 2

Lesson 11

Identifying Parts of a Circle

Identify the parts of the circles below.

1.

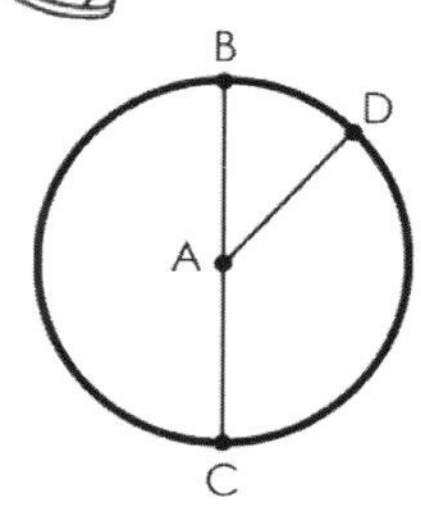

Circle: A

Radius: AB, AC, AD

Diameter: BC

2.

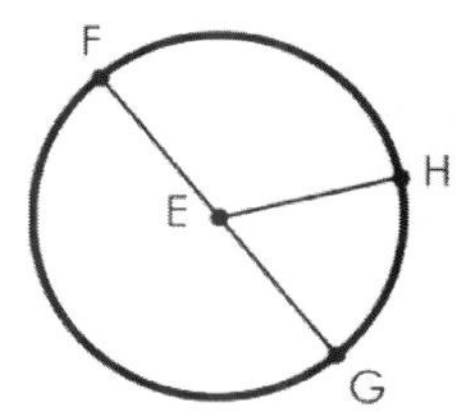

Circle: ______

Radius: ______

Diameter: ______

3.

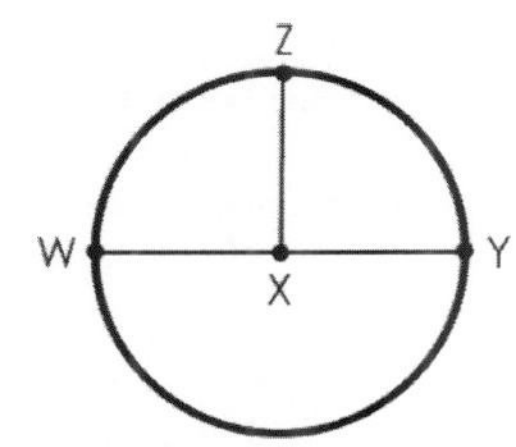

Circle: ______

Radius: ______

Diameter: ______

4.

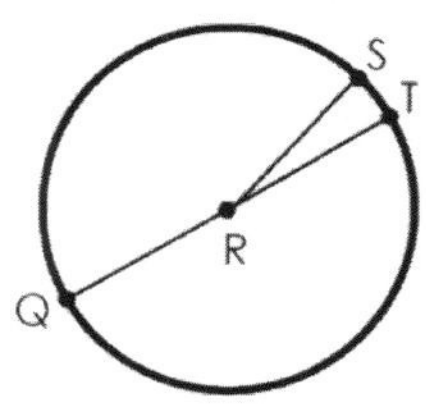

Circle: ______

Radius: ______

Diameter: ______

5.

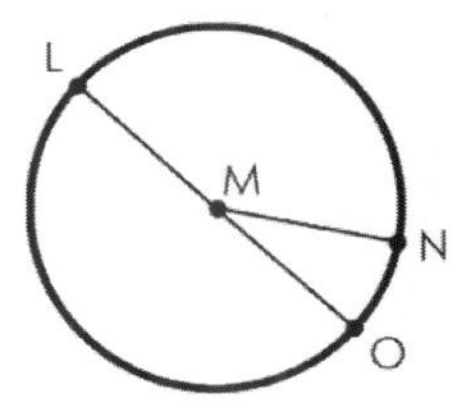

Circle: ______

Radius: ______

Diameter: ______

6.

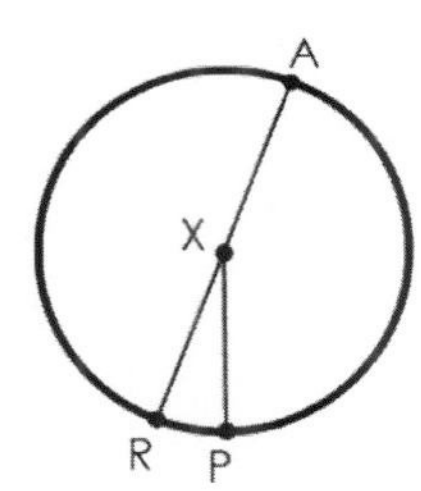

Circle: ______

Radius: ______

Diameter: ______

Lesson 12

Finding the Radius of a Circle

The **radius** of a circle is the distance from the circle's center point to any point on the circle. It can be used to determine a circle's diameter, circumference and area. To find the radius divide the diameter by 2.

Radius = Diameter ÷ 2

Diameter = 12 cm. **Radius** = 6 cm.

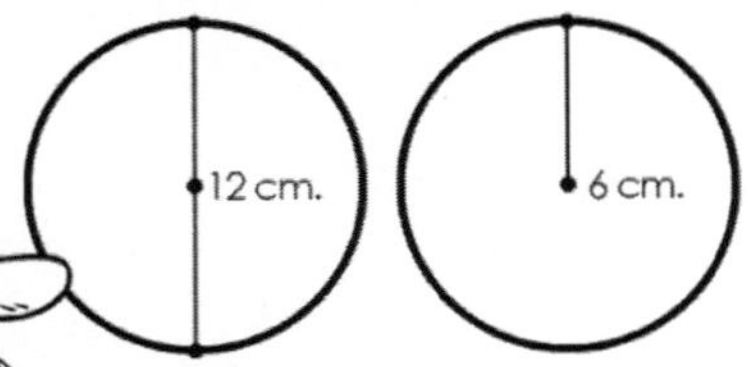

Radius = 12 ÷ 2 = 6 cm.

Using the diameter, determine the radius of each circle.

1. 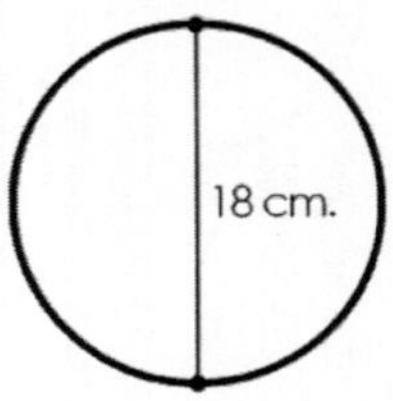

2. 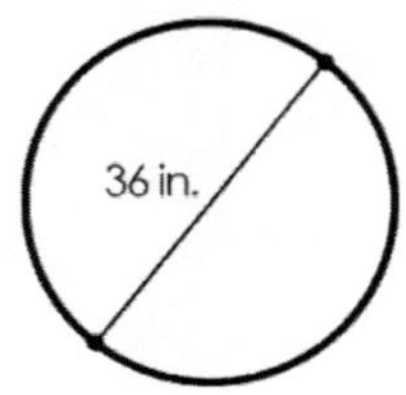

3. 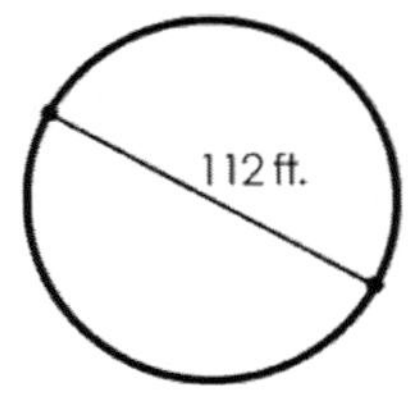

Radius: 18 ÷ 2 = 9 cm. **Radius:** ______________ **Radius:** ______________

4. 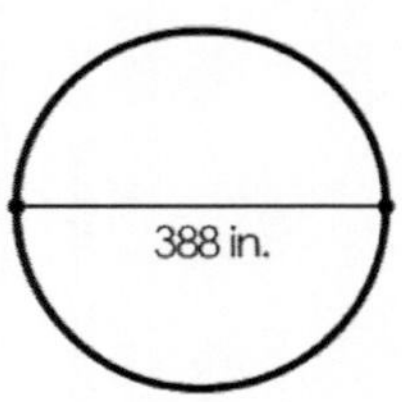

5. 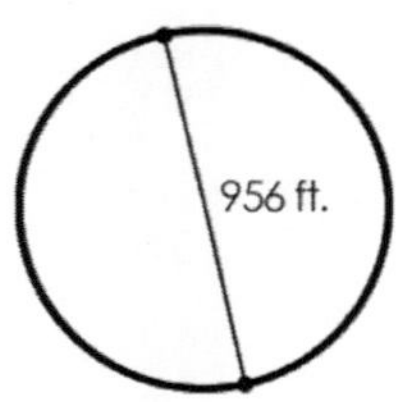

6. 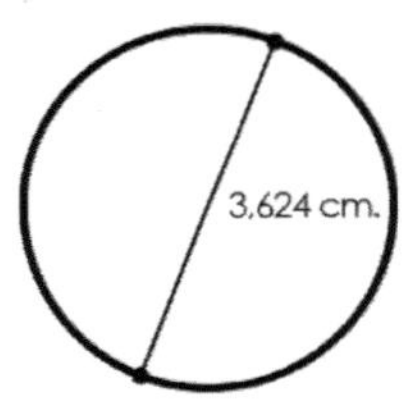

Radius: ______________ **Radius:** ______________ **Radius:** ______________

Lesson 12

Finding the Diameter of a Circle

The **diameter** of a circle is defined as the length of a straight line through the center of a circle and touching two points on its edge, the diameter is twice the measurement of the radius. It is the longest distance across the circle. If the radius of a circle is known, multiplying it by two will equal the diameter.

Diameter = Radius x 2

Radius = 8 cm. **Diameter** = 16 cm.

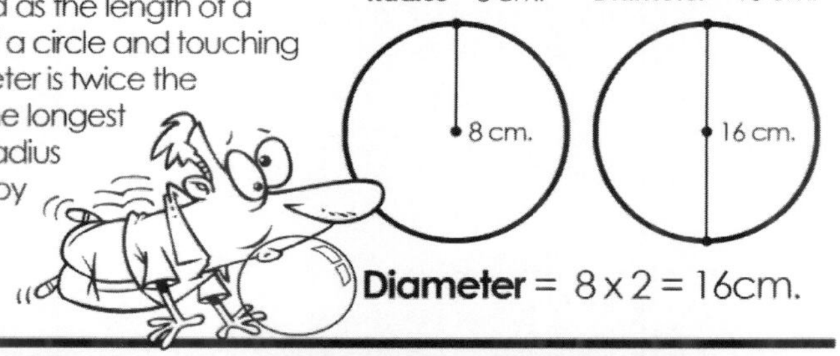

Diameter = 8 x 2 = 16cm.

Using the radius, determine the diameter of each circle.

1.

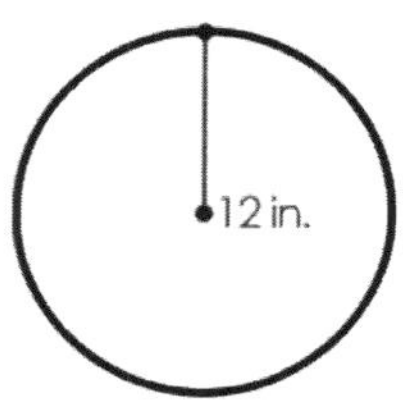

Radius: 12 x 2 = 24 in.

2.

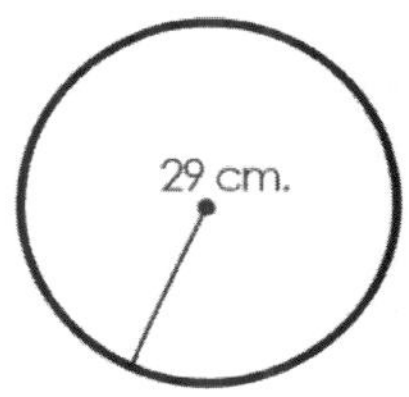

Radius: ______________

3.

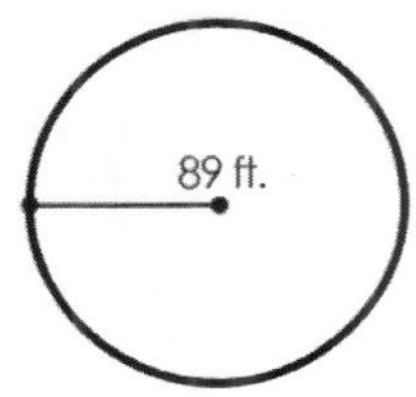

Radius: ______________

4.

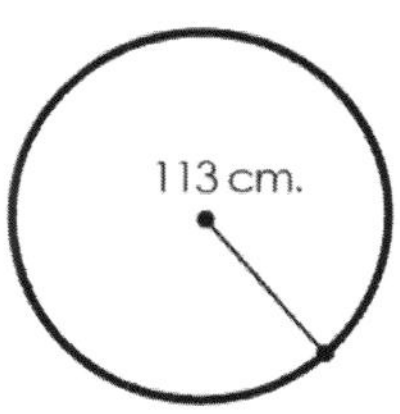

Radius: ______________

5.

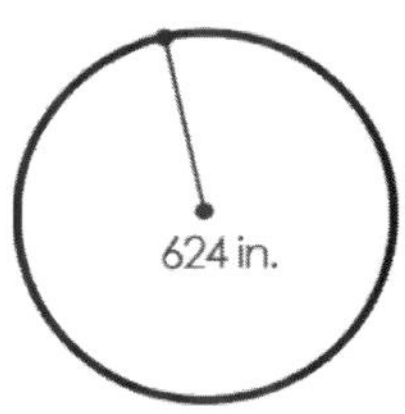

Radius: ______________

6.

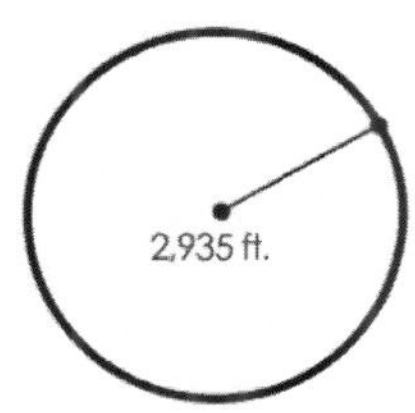

Radius: ______________

Lesson 13

Finding the Circumference of a Circle

A circle's **circumference** is the distance around the circle. To determine the circumference of a circle, multiply the diameter by pi (π), or multiply the radius by 2 then multiply by pi (π). π is a Greek letter used in mathematics to represent 3.14.

Radius = 4 cm. **Diameter** = 8 cm.

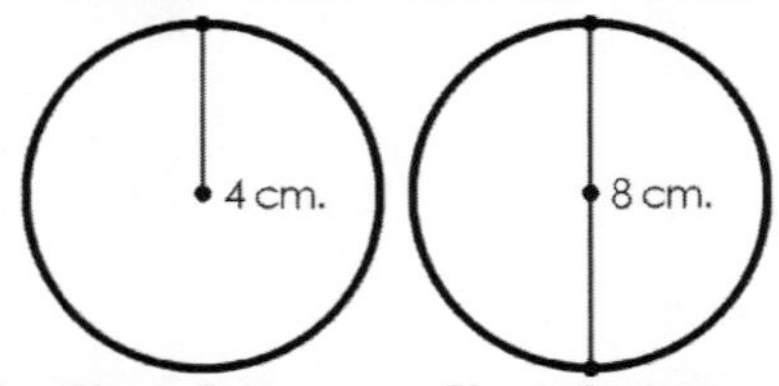

Circumference 4 x 3.14 x 2 = 25.12

Circumference 8 x 3.14 = 25.12

Use these formulas to find the circumference of a circle:
Circumference = (π x diameter) or (π x radius x 2)
Circumference = (3.14 x diameter) or (3.14 x radius x 2)

Using the radius and diameter, determine the circumference of each circle below.

1.

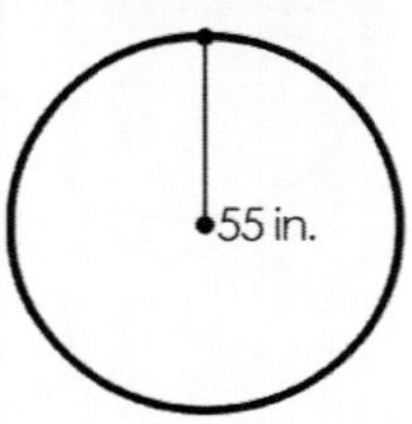

Circumference: 345.4 in.

2.

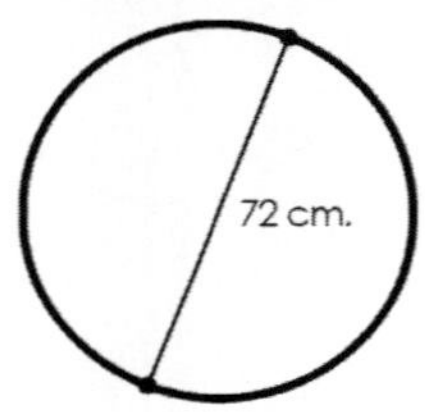

Circumference: ________________

3.

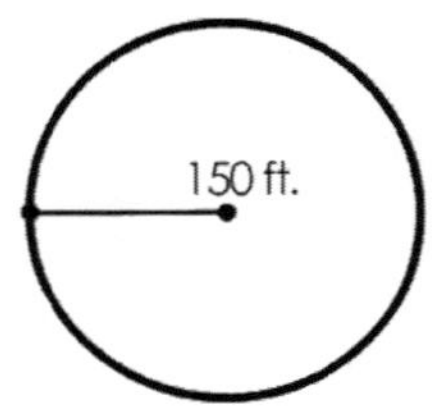

Circumference: ________________

4.

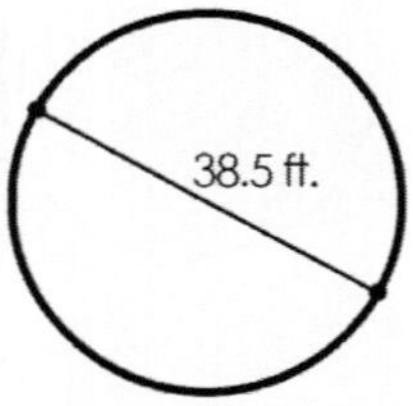

Circumference: ________________

5.

Circumference: ________________

6.

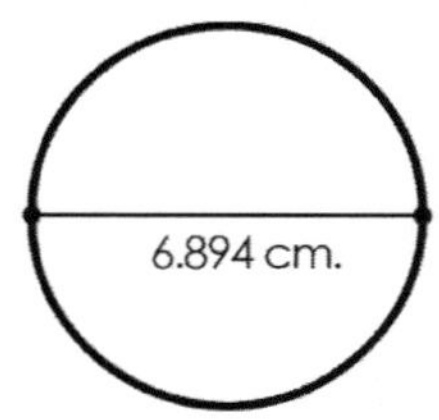

Circumference: ________________

Chapter 7 - Graphs

In this chapter you will learn about the different types of graphs.

You will learn to read and create these types of graphs:

- Bar Graphs
- Line Graphs
- Pie Graphs

Graphs

A graph or chart is a diagram used to display data or information visually. There are three types of graphs: **Bar Graphs**, **Line Graphs** and **Pie Graphs**.

In this chapter you will learn to read and create these types of graphs.

A **bar graph** is useful for comparing facts and comparing quantities in different categories.

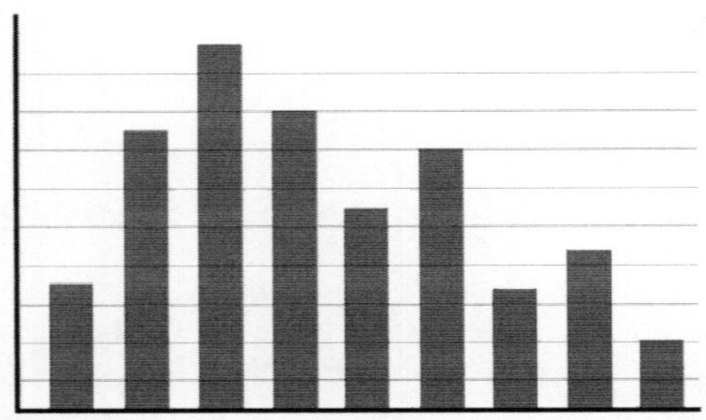

A **line graph** is used to display data or information that changes continuously over time.

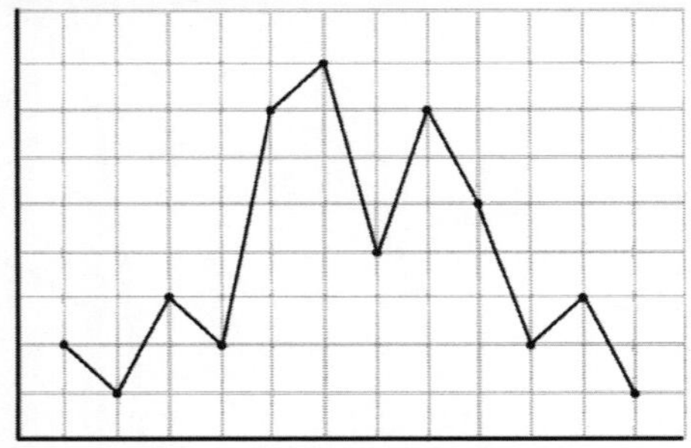

A **pie graph** or **circle graph** shows how the parts of something relate to the whole. It is divided into sectors, where each sector represents a particular category. The sections of this type of graph are usually represented by fractions.

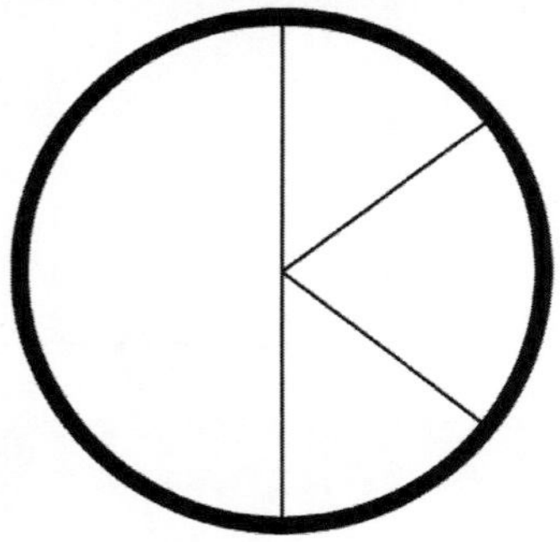

Lesson 1

Reading a Bar Graph 1

Our soccer team did well this year. Here is a graph of the points we scored each game.

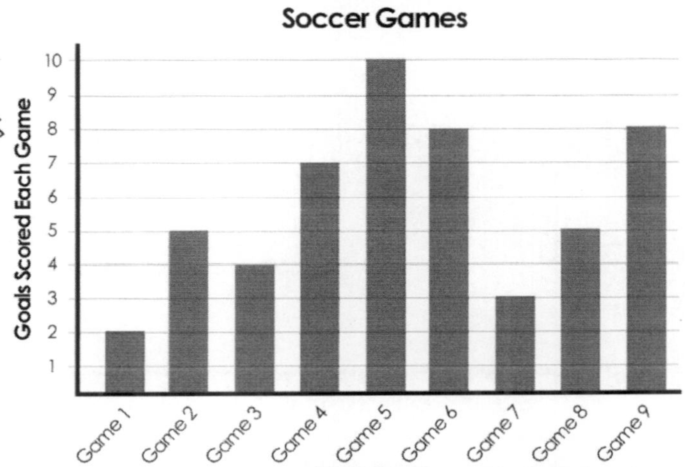

Use the bar graph to answer the questions below.

1. In which game did we score the highest number of goals? ________________
2. In which game did we score the lowest number of goals? ________________
3. How many goals did we score this entire season? ________________
4. In game 9 we scored how many more goals than in game 3? ________________
5. In game 5 we scored how many more goals than in game 7? ________________
6. In games 2, 3 and 4 we scored how many goals in total? ________________
7. In games 4, 5 and 6 we scored how many goals in total? ________________
8. In which games did we score the same number of goals? ________________

Reading a Bar Graph 2

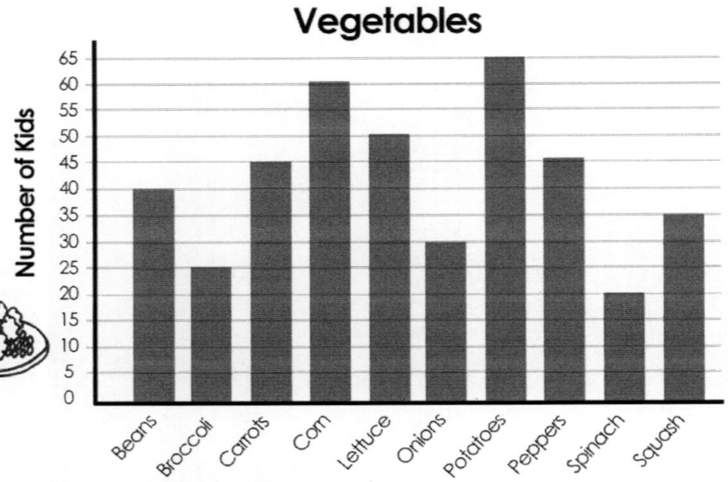

Use the bar graph to answer the questions below.

1. How many kids eat corn? _____

2. How many kids eat squash? _____

3. How many kids eat carrots? _____

4. How many kids eat onions? _____

5. How many kids eat peppers? _____

6. How many kids eat lettuce? _____

7. How many kids eat potatoes? _____

8. How many kids eat broccoli? _____

9. How many kids eat beans? _____

10. How many kids eat spinach? _____

11. How many kids prefer corn over squash? _____

12. How many kids prefer broccoli over spinach? _____

13. How many kids prefer potatoes over beans? _____

14. How many kids prefer lettuce over peppers? _____

15. How many kids prefer carrots over broccoli? _____

16. How many kids prefer corn over onions? _____

17. How many kids prefer potatoes over spinach? _____

18. How many kids prefer beans over onions? _____

Lesson 2

Creating a Bar Graph

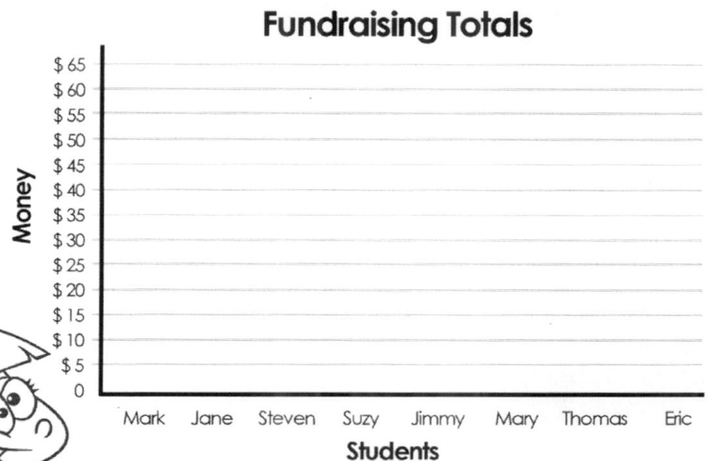

Money raised by each student

Students	Money
Mark	$ 50
Jane	$ 15
Steven	$ 60
Suzy	$ 20
Jimmy	$ 35
Mary	$ 65
Thomas	$ 45
Eric	$ 5

Use the table above to draw the bar graph, then answer the questions below.

1. How much money did Thomas raise? $______

2. How much money did Suzy raise? $______

3. How much money did Jane raise? $______

4. How much money did Jimmy raise? $______

5. How much money did Mark raise? $______

6. How much money did Steven raise? $______

7. How much money did Mary raise? $______

8. How much money did Eric raise? $______

9. Steven raised how much more money than Eric? $______

10. Suzy needs to raise how much more money to catch up with Jimmy? $______

11. Mark needs to raise how much more money to catch up with Mary? $______

12. Steven raised how much more money than Jane ? $______

13. Suzy needs to raise how much more money to catch up with Mary? $______

14. Thomas raised how much more money than Jane? $______

Lesson 3

Comparing Line Graphs

Temperatures in 2011

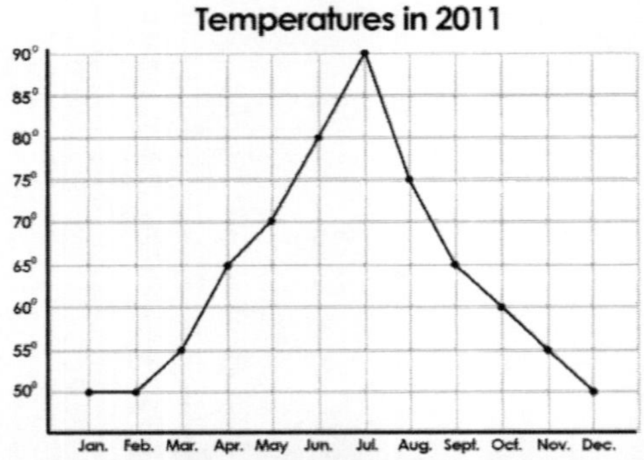

Temperatures in 2012

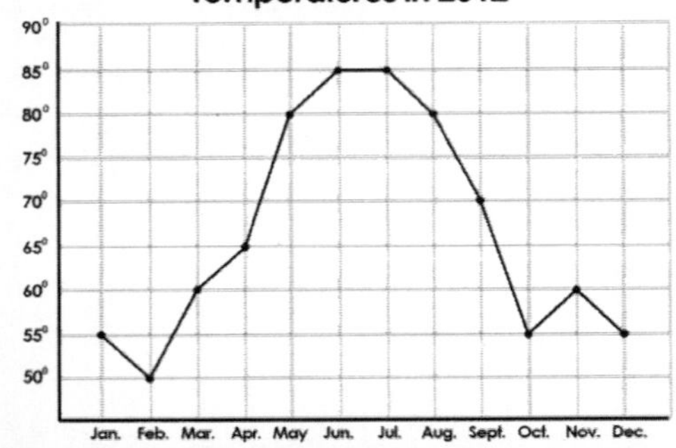

Use the graphs above to answer the questions below.

1. In which year was August hotter? ______________________
2. In which year was December colder? ______________________
3. What was the hottest temperature in 2012? ______________________
4. In 2011 what was the temperature in January? ______________________
5. In 2012 what was the temperature in January? ______________________
6. What was the coldest month in 2012? ______________________
7. What was the hottest month in 2011? ______________________
8. How much cooler was it in January 2011 than it was January in 2012? ______________
9. What was the hottest temperature in 2011? ______________________
10. In 2011 what was the temperature in October? ______________________
11. In 2012 what was the temperature in October? ______________________
12. How much hotter was it in May 2012 than it was May in 2011? ______________
13. Compared to April 2011, did the temperature rise, fall, or stay the same in April 2012? ______________
14. Which year had the highest temperature? ______________________

Lesson 4

Creating a Line Graph

Line graphs use points and lines to show data visually.

Use the data on the left to draw your own line graph.
First plot the points, then draw a line connecting the points

Numbers of People in Museum	
Time	**People**
9 am	20
10 am	55
11 am	30
12 pm	10
1 pm	45
2 pm	65
3 pm	60
4 pm	40
5 pm	55
6 pm	15

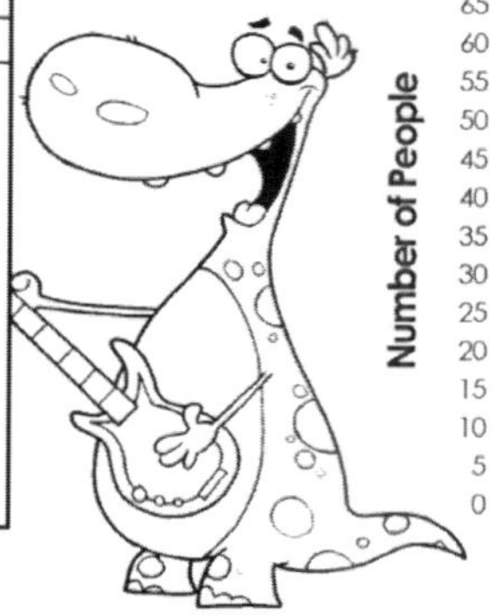

Museum Attendance

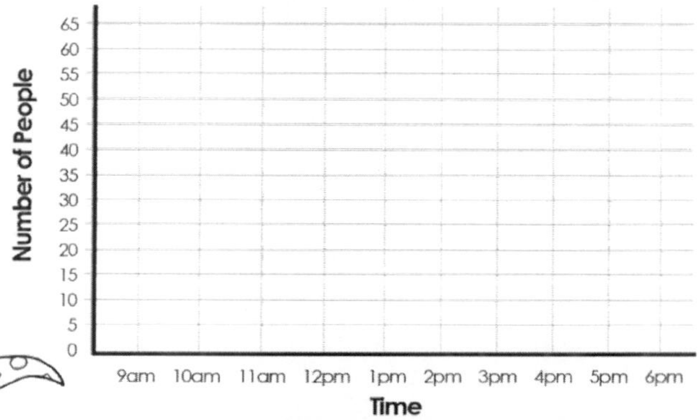

Use the line graph you just drew to answer the questions below.

1. At what time was the attendance in the museum the highest? ____________
2. At what time was the attendance in the museum the lowest? ____________
3. How many people were in the museum at noon? ____________
4. How many people were in the museum at 9am? ____________
5. How many people were in the museum at 4pm? ____________
6. How many more people were the in the museum at 5pm compared to 11am? ____________
7. From 1pm to 2pm, how many people showed up at the museum? ____________
8. From 5pm to 6pm, how many people left the museum? ____________
9. During what one-hour time period did the attendance increase the most? ____________
10. During what one-hour time period did the attendance decrease the most? ____________

Lesson 5

Identifying Points on a Graph

Graphs are used to show information in a visual form.

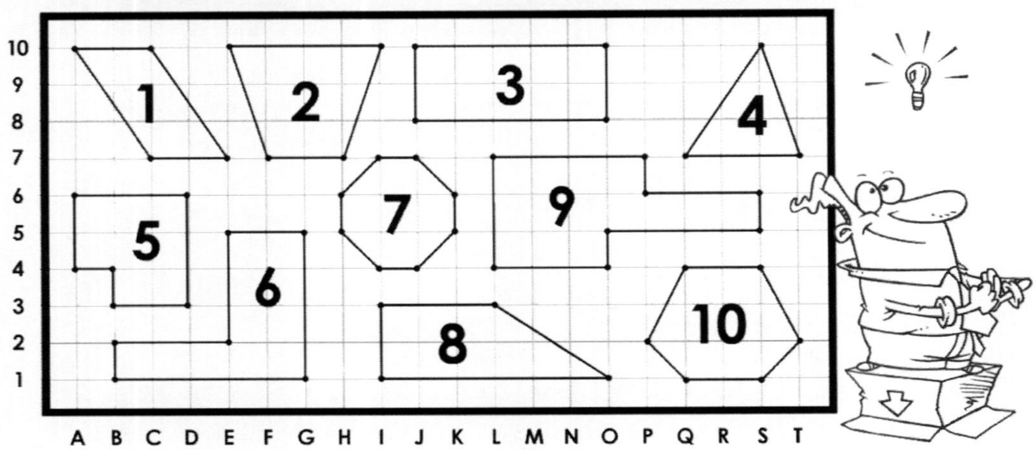

Using the graph above, write out the points that make up each shape.

1. A10, C10, C7, E7 ______________

2. ______________

3. ______________

4. ______________

5. ______________

6. ______________

7. ______________

8. ______________

9. ______________

10. ______________

Lesson 6

Plotting Points on a Graph

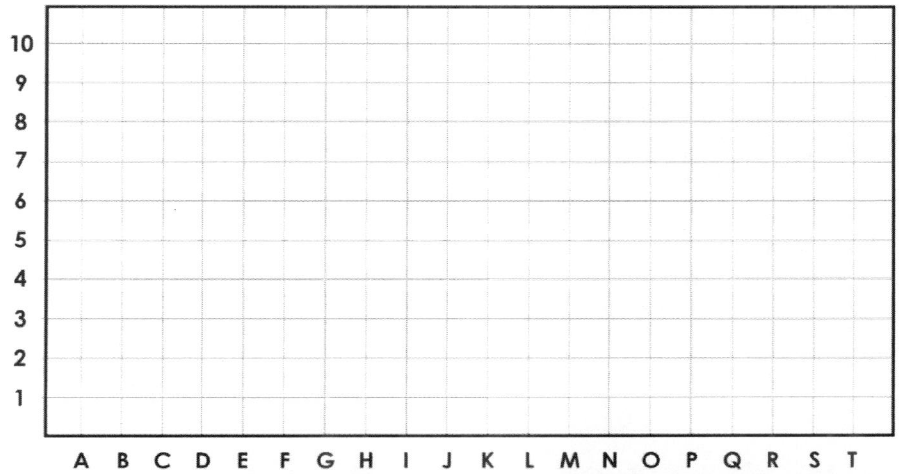

Using the coordinates below, plot the points on the graph above.
Draw a line between the points on the graph to create geometric shapes and the write the name for each shape in the blanks.

1. A4, B1, E1, F4 trapezoid
2. G3, i3, G1, i1 ________________
3. H6, L6, H4, L4 ________________
4. P7, R10, T7 ________________
5. F7, i10, L10, i7 ________________
6. N8, M5, N2, O5 ________________
7. P4, R5, T4, Q1, S1 ________________

Lesson 7

Reading a Pie Chart 1

A **pie graph** shows how the parts of something relate to the whole.
It is divided into sectors. Each sector represents a particular category.

Use the graphs below to answer the questions.

Students' Favorite Classes

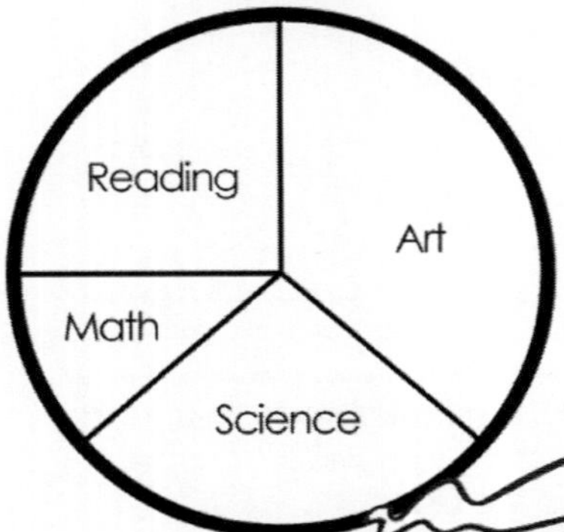

1. Which class do the students like most?

____

2. Which class do the students like the least?

____

3. What is the second-favorite class?

____

4. Which class do the students like more, math or reading?

____

Kids' Favorite Pets

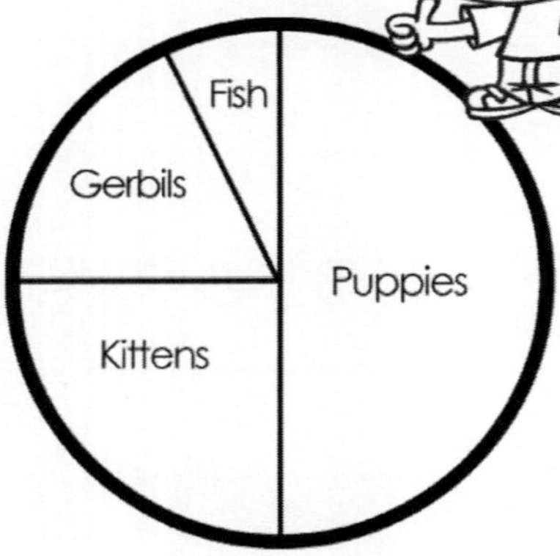

5. What is the kids' favorite pet?

____

6. What is the kids' least favorite pet?

____

7. What is the kids' second favorite pet?

____

8. Do more kids' want a gerbil or fish?

____

Lesson 8

Reading a Pie Chart 2a

Shoe types that family members prefer.

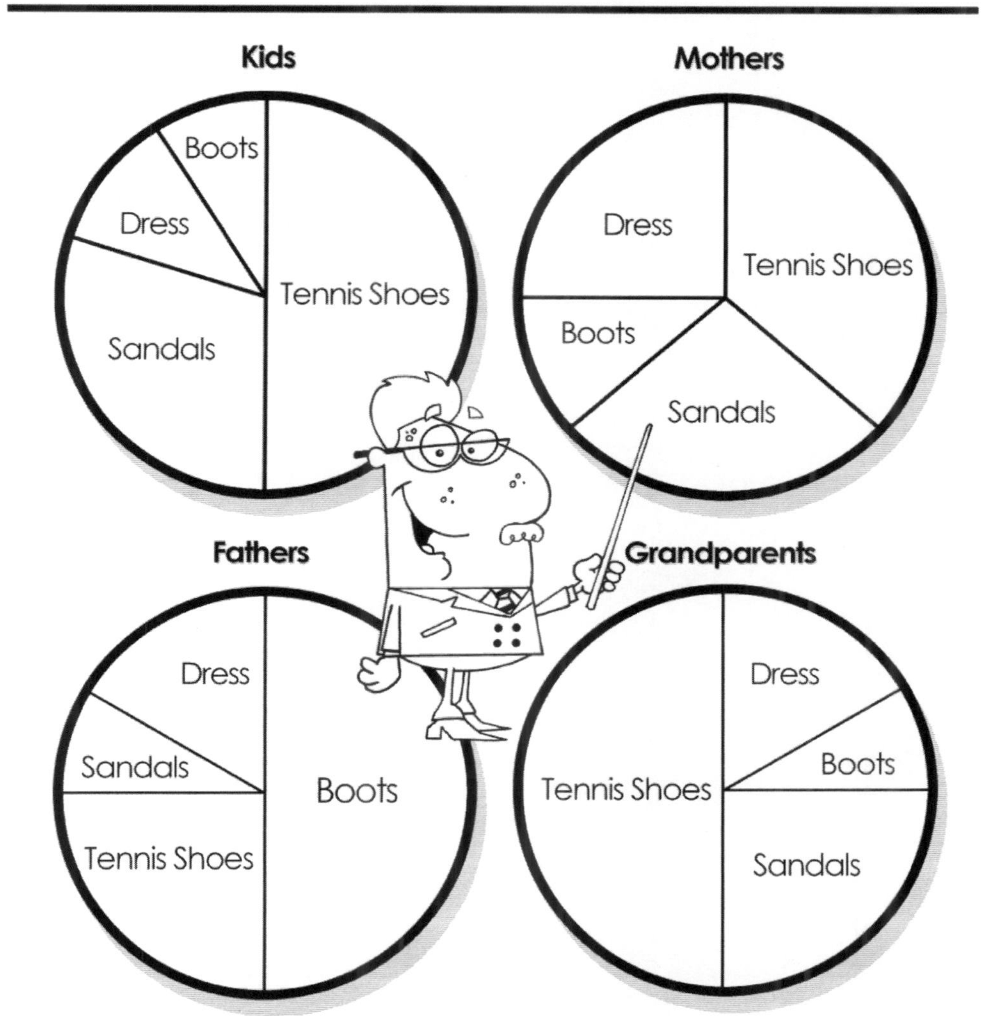

Lesson 9

Reading a Pie Chart 2b

Use the pie charts on the last page to answer the questions below.

1. Which shoes do kids like the most? ______________________
2. Which shoes do grandparents like the most? ______________________
3. Which shoes do mothers like the most? ______________________
4. Which shoes do fathers like the most? ______________________
5. What is the kids' second favorite shoes? ______________________
6. What is the fathers' second favorite shoes? ______________________
7. Which shoes do kids like least? ______________________
8. Which shoes do grandparents like least? ______________________
9. Which shoes do mothers like least? ______________________
10. Which shoes do fathers like least? ______________________

Lesson 10

Creating a Pie Chart

A **pie graph** shows how the parts of something relate to the whole. It is divided into sectors. Each sector represents a particular category. The sum of all the parts will always equal 100%.

Using the information below, fill in the pie graphs with the correct numbers.

Most Studied Planets

1. Mars - 50%
2. Mercury - 6%
3. Venus - 10%
4. Neptune - 34%

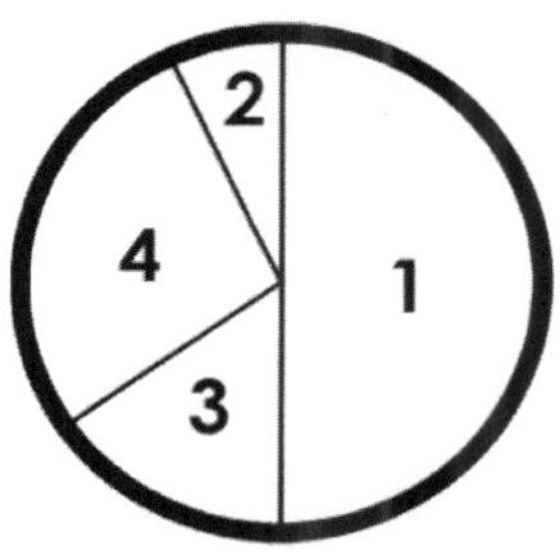

How Students Get to School

1. School Bus - 42%
2. Car - 35%
3. Bike - 15%
4. Walk - 8%

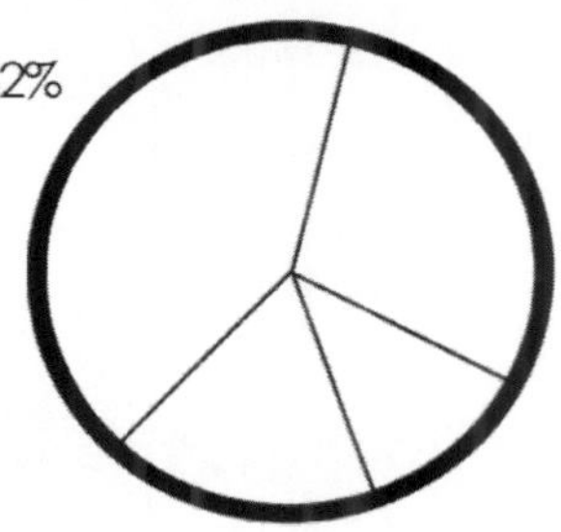

Favorite Movie Types in Schools

1. Comedy - 35%
2. Action - 18%
3. Drama - 8%
4. Animation - 24%
5. Science Fiction- 15%

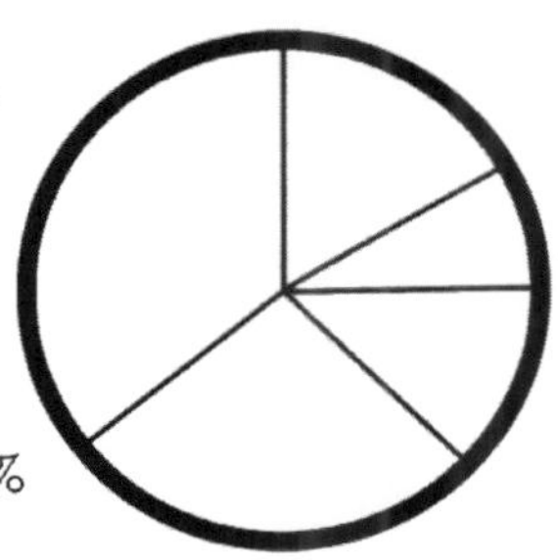

Fish Population in the Pond

1. Bass - 20%
2. Catfish - 27%
3. Trout - 14%
4. Guppies - 32%
5. Turtles - 7%

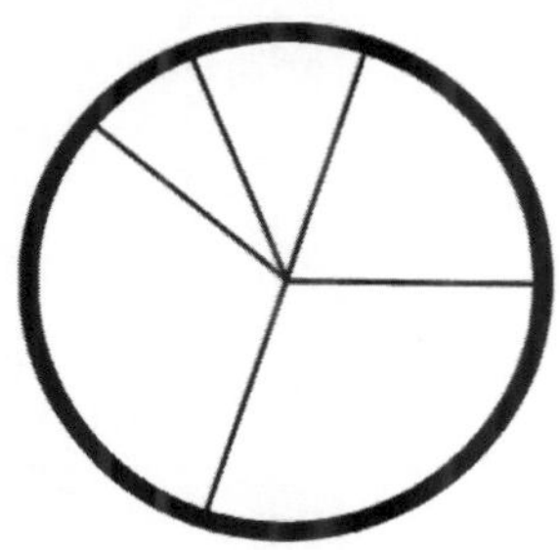

Practice Test #1

Practice Questions

1. What is the value of the digit 5 in the number 3,456,789?

Ⓐ Fifty thousand

Ⓑ Five thousand

Ⓒ Five-hundred thousand

Ⓓ Five million

2. In ice hockey, the number of points a player scores is defined as the sum of the number of goals and the number of assists. Which hockey player listed in the table below has the highest number of points?

Player	Goals	Assists
Phillips	2	23
Jackson	5	17
Robinson	13	15
Miller	8	19

Ⓐ Phillips

Ⓑ Jackson

Ⓒ Robinson

Ⓓ Miller

3. A recipe calls for $3\frac{3}{4}$ cups of flour. Which fraction below is equivalent to this amount?

Ⓐ $\frac{5}{2}$

Ⓑ $\frac{15}{4}$

Ⓒ $\frac{3}{2}$

Ⓓ $\frac{9}{4}$

4. One morning a total of 151 eggs are collected from a henhouse. The eggs are packed in cartons of 12 for shipment. How many eggs are remaining after as many cartons as possible are packed?

Ⓐ 3

Ⓑ 9

Ⓒ 7

Ⓓ 1

5. Which numeral is in the thousandths place in 0.3874?

Ⓐ 3

Ⓑ 8

Ⓒ 7

Ⓓ 4

6. A rectangular plot in a garden is three times longer than it is wide. What is the perimeter of the garden if it has a width of 8 meters?

Ⓐ 32 meters

Ⓑ 192 meters

Ⓒ 24 meters

Ⓓ 64 meters

7. Part A: The number of customers in a new restaurant is given in the table below:

Week	Customers
1	155
2	180
3	205

How many customers should be expected in week 4?

Ⓐ 225

Ⓑ 230

Ⓒ 200

Ⓓ 255

Part B: The average meal at the restaurant is $12. How much money will they make in week 4?

____

8. The rectangular prism below has a volume of 144 cu. cm. The length and width are given below. What is the height of the rectangular prism?

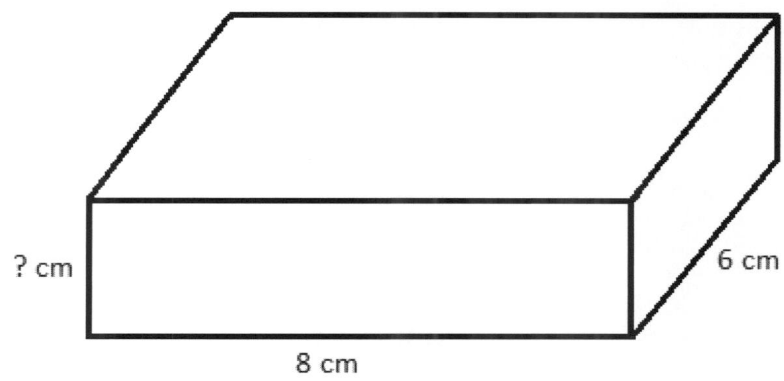

---

9. 0.58 - 0.39=

Ⓐ 0.19

Ⓑ 1.9

Ⓒ 0.29

Ⓓ 2.9

10. The recipe Mary is using to bake cupcakes requires 1 cup of milk and makes 8 cupcakes. If she needs to make 32 cupcakes for the party, how much milk is needed?

Ⓐ 1 pint

Ⓑ 1 gallon

Ⓒ 3 cups

Ⓓ 1 quart

11. Solve the equation: $\frac{2}{5} + \frac{3}{4} - \frac{1}{2} = ?$

____

12. Which of the following is correct?

Ⓐ $\frac{4}{7} = \frac{12}{21}$

Ⓑ $\frac{3}{4} = \frac{12}{20}$

Ⓒ $\frac{5}{8} = \frac{15}{32}$

Ⓓ $\frac{7}{9} = \frac{28}{35}$

13. Donnie has a baseball card that is 4.2 inches tall and 2.6 inches wide. What is the area of the card?

____

14. An electronics store sells *E* Evercell brand batteries in packages of 4 and *D* Durapower brand batteries in packages of 6. Which expression represents the total number of batteries in the store?

Ⓐ $(4 + E) \times (6 + D)$

Ⓑ $(4 \times E) + (6 \times D)$

Ⓒ $(4 + E) + (6 + D)$

Ⓓ $(4 \times E) \div (6 \times D)$

15. At the park there is a walking trail that goes around the perimeter. One lap around the park is .28 miles. Samantha walks 11 laps. How far has she walked?

____

16. Solve the equations below:

$.3 \times 1.25 = ?$

$1.22 - .85 + .34 = ?$

$(.22 + 1.48) \times .5 = ?$

17. Given the figure of the parallelogram below, which side is parallel to side $\overline{RT}$?

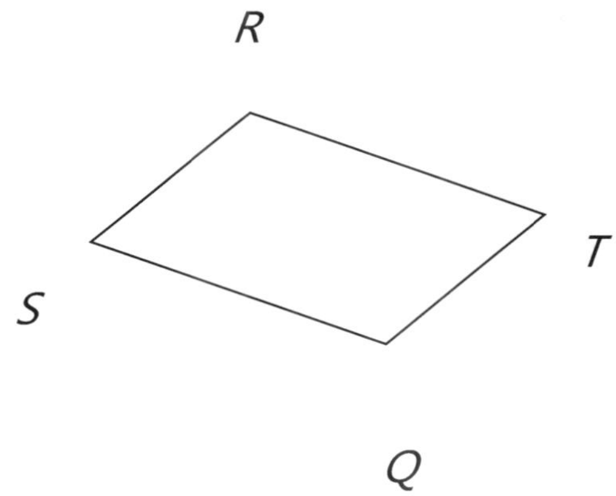

Ⓐ $\overline{RS}$

Ⓑ $\overline{QS}$

Ⓒ $\overline{QT}$

Ⓓ None of the above

18. A fish tank is a rectangular prism with a length of 7 inches and a width of 5 inches and can hold a volume of 210 cubic inches of water. What is the height of the tank?

Ⓐ 6 inches

Ⓑ 5 inches

Ⓒ 17.5 inches

Ⓓ 10 inches

19. The all-time rushing leader in professional football ran for 18,335 yards in his career. What is the best whole number approximation of the number of miles he ran?

____

20. A survey of a random sample of 100 drivers asked them the color of their car. The results of the survey are presented in the table below.

Color of car	Number of drivers
Blue	26
Red	14
Yellow	36
Silver	24

If the parking lot at the local store is filled with 25 cars, how many yellow cars would be expected to be in the lot?

Ⓐ 6

Ⓑ 9

Ⓒ 11

Ⓓ 12

21. Cindy earned $100 one week at the ice cream stand. She put $\frac{1}{4}$ of the money in her savings account and kept the rest as cash. After this, she received a cash bonus of $20 from the owner of the ice cream stand and didn't put any of it in the savings account. Which expression represents the amount of cash Cindy currently has?

Ⓐ $C = \frac{3}{4}(100) + 20$

Ⓑ $C = \frac{1}{4}(100) + 20$

Ⓒ $C = \frac{1}{4}(100) - 20$

Ⓓ $C = \frac{3}{4}(120)$

22. Mr. Thompson fills his 25.2 gallon gasoline tank with gas that costs $2.98 a gallon. Which is the best approximation of the cost of the gasoline?

Ⓐ $50

Ⓑ $60

Ⓒ $75

Ⓓ $90

23. Using the order of operations solve the problem below.

$8 \times (5 - 2) + (4 + 5) =$ ____________________

24. Janice gets home from school at 2:45 PM. She does homework for 1 hour and 30 minutes, then goes out and plays for 1 hour and 45 minutes before returning home for dinner. What time is it when Janice returns home for dinner?

Ⓐ 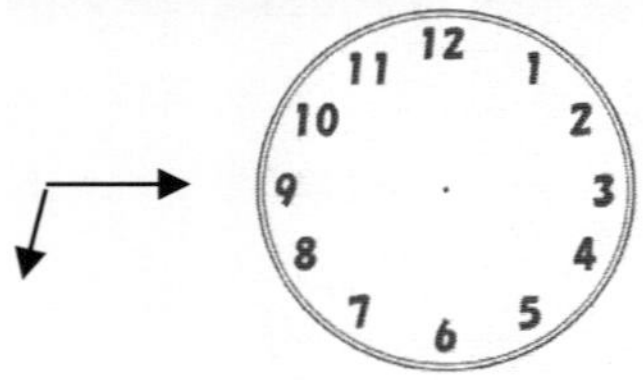

Ⓑ 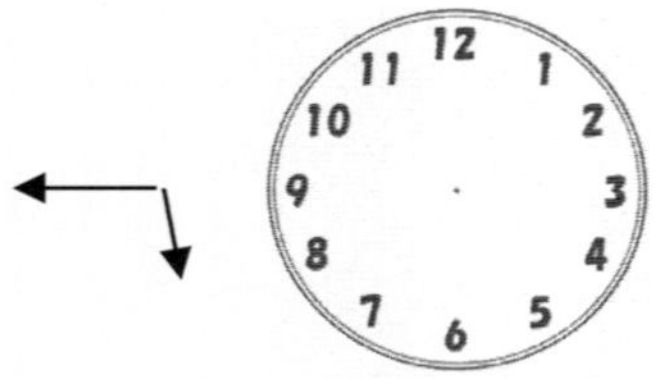

Ⓒ 

Ⓓ 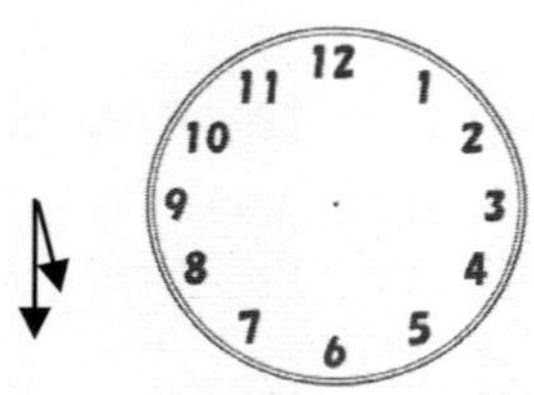

25. Two sisters were arguing who could have a larger piece of pie. Their mother told the older daughter she could have 2/5 of the pie. She told the younger daughter she could have 1/3 of the pie. Which daughter received a larger piece of pie?

Ⓐ The older daughter.

Ⓑ The younger daughter

Ⓒ Same size piece for each daughter

Ⓓ Not enough information to determine

26. It takes Jack 14.67 minutes to get to school in the morning. It only takes Clayton 10.24 minutes to get to school. How much less time does it take Jack to get to school?

____

27. A ship is located on the map at coordinates (4, 9). If the radar indicates the lighthouse is 5 units east and 4 units south of the ship, what is the location of the lighthouse?

Nort

Ⓐ (9,
5)
Ⓑ (9,
4)
Ⓒ (8.

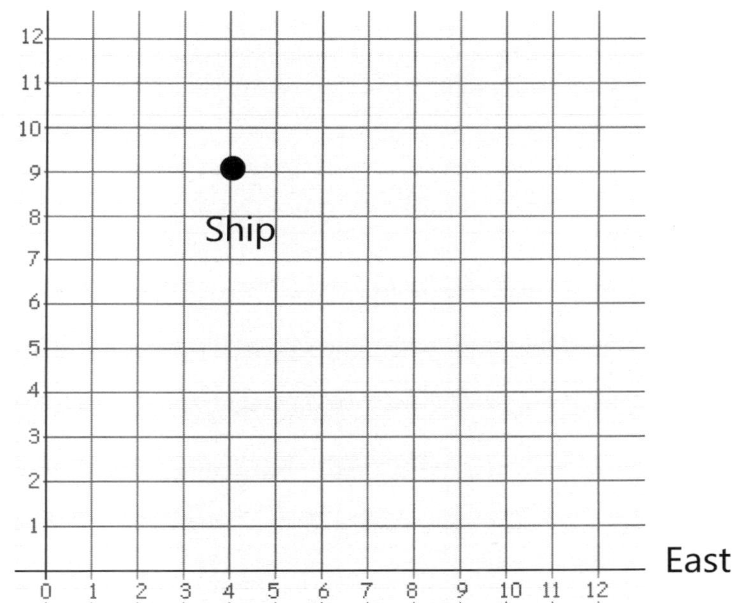

28. When taking a person's temperature with an oral thermometer, temperatures between 96.9° and 99.5° are considered normal. Which temperature below is outside of the normal range?

Ⓐ 97.2°

Ⓑ 99.3°

Ⓒ 98.9°

Ⓓ 96.3°

29. The high temperatures in degrees Celsius for a work week are given on the table below:

Day	Monday	Tuesday	Wednesday	Thursday	Friday
High Temp.	9	16	13	20	22

What was the mean high temperature for the week?

Ⓐ 14

Ⓑ 16

Ⓒ 13

Ⓓ 22

30. On the graph below plot the points (6,9), (3,8), and (-2,4).

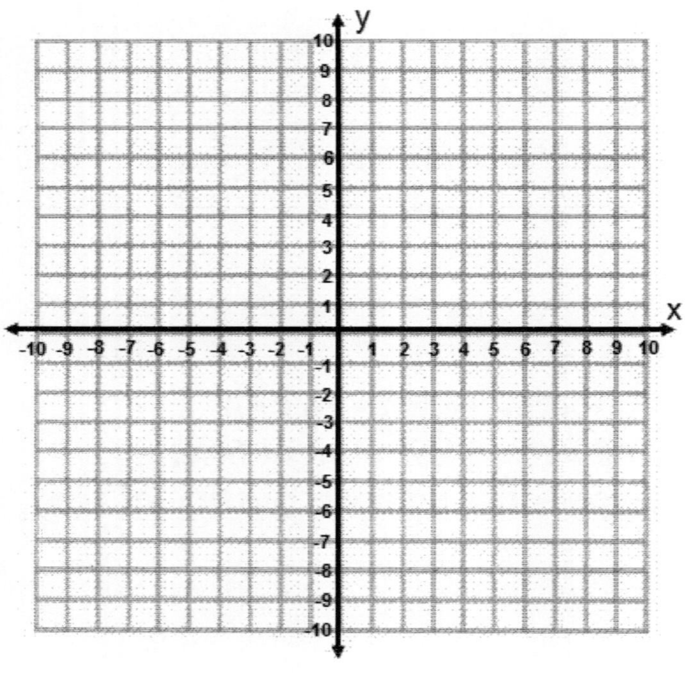

31. A little league has 92 children sign up for baseball season. If each team needs at least 14 players, how many complete baseball teams can be formed?

Ⓐ 5

Ⓑ 6

Ⓒ 7

Ⓓ 8

32. Part A: Given the isosceles trapezoid PQRS below, which two sides are congruent?

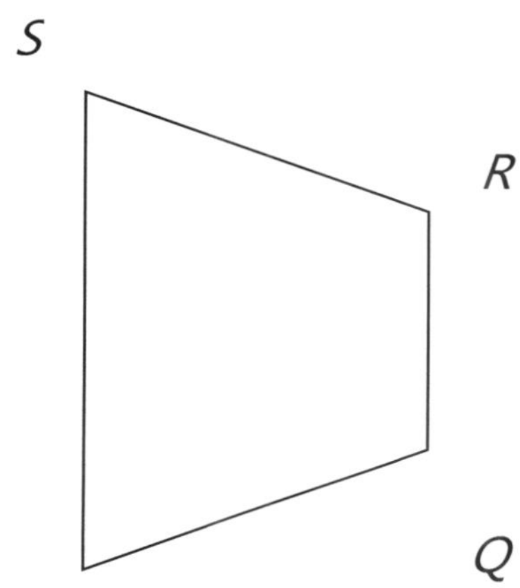

Ⓐ $\overline{PS}$ and $\overline{QR}$

Ⓑ $\overline{RS}$ and $\overline{QF}$ P

Ⓒ $\overline{QP}$ and $\overline{RQ}$

Ⓓ $\overline{PS}$ and $\overline{RS}$

Part B: Which two sides are parallel?

Ⓐ $\overline{PS}$ and $\overline{QR}$

Ⓑ $\overline{RS}$ and $\overline{QF}$ P

Ⓒ $\overline{QP}$ and $\overline{RQ}$

Ⓓ $\overline{PS}$ and $\overline{RS}$

33. A length of string is measured to be $\frac{31}{8}$ inches. Between which two points on the ruler below will this length lie?

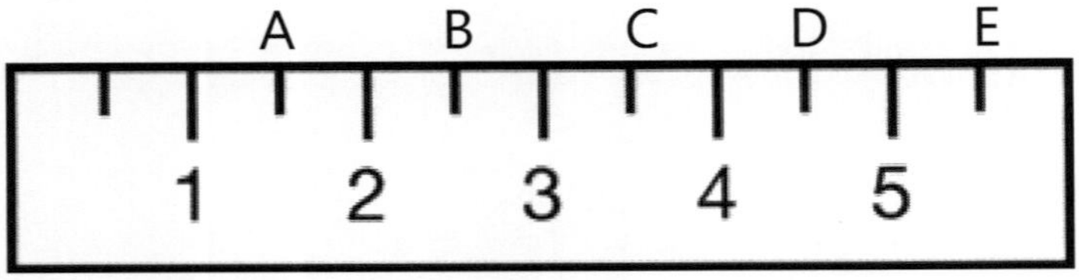

Ⓐ Between points A and B

Ⓑ Between points B and C

Ⓒ Between points C and D

Ⓓ Between points D and E

34. Which point lies within the shaded region below?

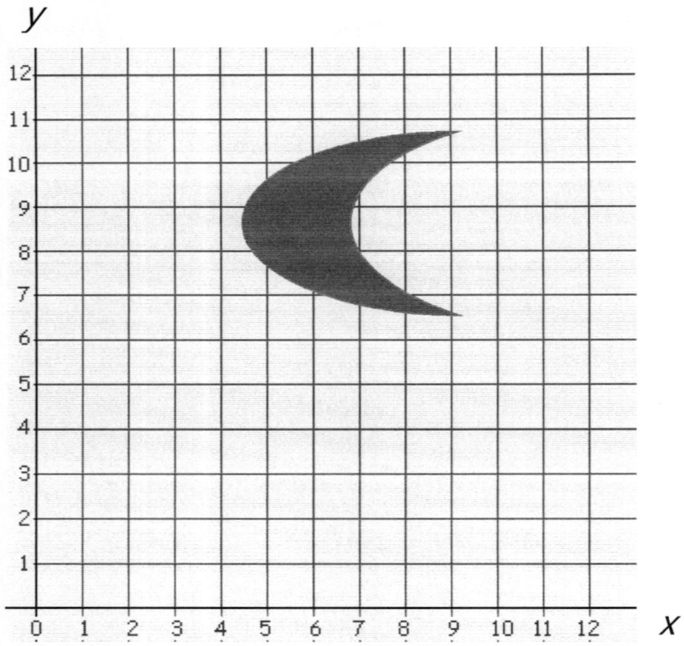

Ⓐ (5, 6)

Ⓑ (8, 6)

Ⓒ (7, 10)

Ⓓ (9, 9)

35. The model shown below represents $1\frac{7}{10}$

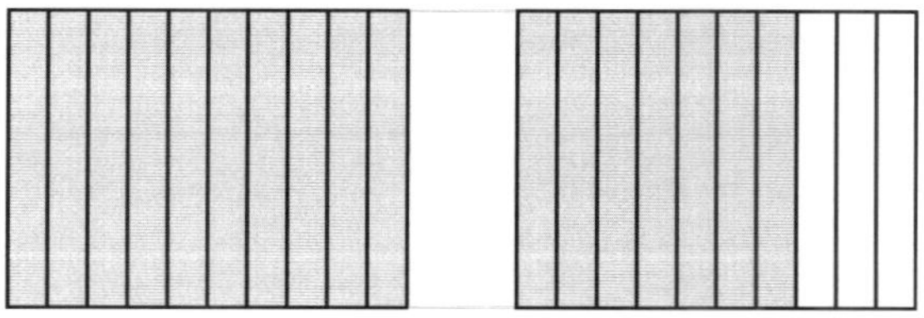

Which decimal does this also represent?

Ⓐ 0.7

Ⓑ 0.07

Ⓒ 1.7

Ⓓ 1.07

36. An electronics store sells T.V.'s for \$525 and game systems for \$250. If 36 people buy T.V. and 29 people buy a game system how much money would the store make?

____

37. Of the 20 people in Joan's class, 4 of them have birthdays in the winter, 7 have birthdays in the spring, 3 have birthdays in the summer, and 6 have birthdays in the fall. What is the probability a student chosen at random will have a birthday in either the spring or the summer?

Ⓐ $\frac{7}{20}$

Ⓑ $\frac{1}{2}$

Ⓒ $\frac{3}{20}$

Ⓓ $\frac{3}{10}$

38. Phil is going to school overseas for 9 weeks and 5 days. How many days will Phil be gone?

Ⓐ 95

Ⓑ 44

Ⓒ 59

Ⓓ 68

39. Julie shopped for first-aid cream. One large tube held 1.5 fluid ounces and the smallest tube held 0.33 fluid ounces. What is the difference in the number of fluid ounces of cream in the two tubes?

Ⓐ 1.8

Ⓑ 1.27

Ⓒ 1.23

Ⓓ 1.17

40. Jan played a game which used a fair spinner like the one shown here. Jan needs the arrow to land on green on her next turn.

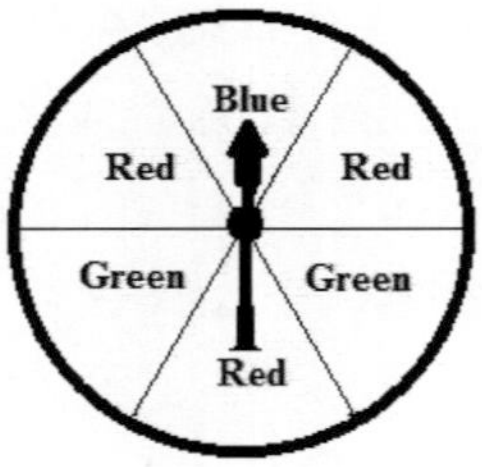

What is the probability that the arrow lands on green when Jan spins one time?

Ⓐ $\frac{1}{6}$

Ⓑ $\frac{1}{3}$

Ⓒ $\frac{1}{2}$

Ⓓ $\frac{2}{3}$

Practice Test #2

Practice Questions

1. Which number represents "fifty-seven thousand three hundred and forty"?

Ⓐ 570,340

Ⓑ 573,400

Ⓒ 5,734

Ⓓ 57,340

2. Four students were given a typing test measuring their speed in words per minute and then given the same typing test several weeks later. Which student had the greatest improvement?

Student	First score (words per minute)	Second score (words per minute)
Alexander	22	39
Betty	39	48
Carolyn	27	43
David	22	42

Ⓐ Alexander

Ⓑ Betty

Ⓒ Carolyn

Ⓓ David

3. A bookshelf is to be $7\frac{5}{8}$ inches wide. Which fraction below is equivalent to this measurement?

Ⓐ $\frac{35}{8}$

Ⓑ $\frac{75}{8}$

Ⓒ $\frac{61}{8}$

Ⓓ $\frac{43}{8}$

4. Toasty Donut Shop makes 141 donuts one morning. The donuts are packaged in boxes of 12 for delivery. How many single donuts are left over?

Ⓐ 3

Ⓑ 9

Ⓒ 6

Ⓓ 1

5. Which numeral is in the thousandths place in .5643?

Ⓐ 5

Ⓑ 6

Ⓒ 4

Ⓓ 3

6. Dennis weighs 56 pounds. His little brother Donny weighs 23 pounds less than him. What is Donny's weight in ounces?

____

7. A square flower garden has an area of 81 feet. What is the length of one side of the garden?

Ⓐ 9 feet

Ⓑ 20.25 feet

Ⓒ 40.5 feet

Ⓓ 324 feet

8. Which of the following is correct?

Ⓐ $\frac{2}{3} = \frac{18}{24}$

Ⓑ $\frac{4}{5} = \frac{16}{20}$

Ⓒ $\frac{1}{9} = \frac{4}{18}$

Ⓓ $\frac{3}{8} = \frac{9}{16}$

9. Round each of the decimals below to the nearest hundredth.

$3.116 \approx$ ________

$3.081 \approx$ ________

$3.006 \approx$ ________

$3.107 \approx$ ________

10. Which of the following figures is a trapezoid?

Ⓐ 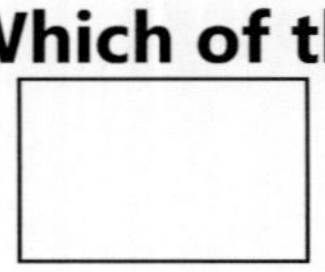

Ⓑ 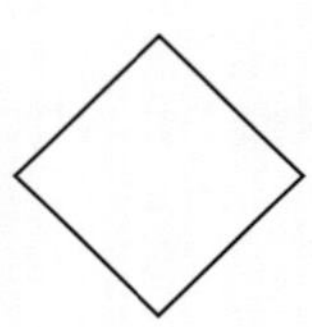

Ⓒ 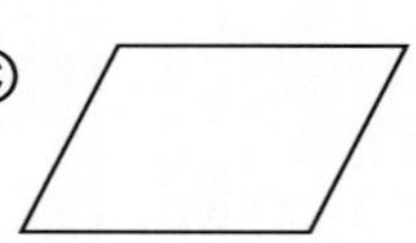

Ⓓ 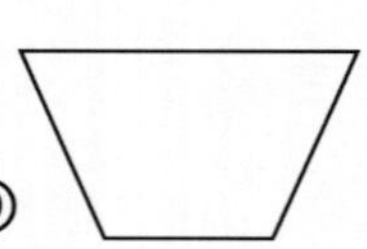

11. A gallon of cooking oil is used to make popcorn for 256 people. How much cooking oil is needed to make popcorn for 96 people?

Ⓐ 2 quarts

Ⓑ 3 pints

Ⓒ 1 quart

Ⓓ 1 cup

12. Jodi made a sum of money yesterday at a bake sale. She spent half of the money to buy more ingredients for next week's bake sale, and then spent \$12 to go to the movies. Jodi has \$17 remaining. How much did she make yesterday at the bake sale?

Ⓐ \$36

Ⓑ \$58

Ⓒ \$46

Ⓓ \$41

13. Express 99/14 as a mixed fraction.

Ⓐ $7\frac{1}{14}$

Ⓑ $7\frac{3}{14}$

Ⓒ $7\frac{11}{14}$

Ⓓ $7\frac{5}{14}$

14. A little boy decides to give away all of his marbles. Each of his 4 friends is to receive an equal share. Which of the statements below describes how this can be done?

Ⓐ Multiply his marbles by 4 and give this amount to each of his friends

Ⓑ Multiply his marbles by 2 and give this amount to each of his friends

Ⓒ Multiply his marbles by 1/2 and give this amount to each of his friends

Ⓓ Multiply his marbles by 1/4 and give this amount to each of his friends

15. Part A: A store receives regular shipments of paper towels. Each shipment contains 26 boxes. Each box contains 6 packages and each package has 8 rolls of paper towels. How many rolls of paper towels come in one shipment?

____

Part B: If the store sells 6100 rolls each month how many shipments will it need in one month?

____

16. Part A: A zoo has three different lion enclosures. The first one is $\frac{5}{8}$ of an acre. The second one is $\frac{5}{6}$ of an acre. How much bigger is the second one than the first one?

____

Part B: If the third one is $\frac{7}{12}$, what is the total number of acres in all three enclosures?

____

17. Given the figure of the parallelogram below, which side is congruent to side $\overline{RT}$?

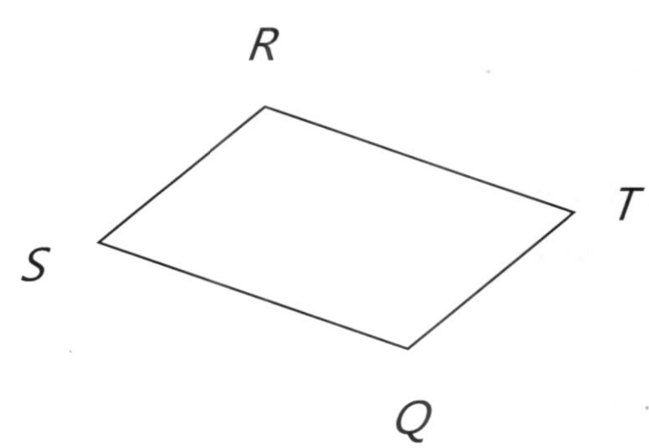

Ⓐ $\overline{RS}$

Ⓑ $\overline{QS}$

Ⓒ $\overline{QT}$

Ⓓ None of the above

18. A large rectangular-prism-shaped tank at the zoo is 8 feet wide and 5 feet high. How long is the tank if it holds a volume of 200 cubic feet of water?

Ⓐ 8 feet

Ⓑ 6 feet

Ⓒ 13 feet

Ⓓ 5 feet

19. Mount McKinley, the tallest mountain in North America, is 20,320 feet high. Approximately how many miles tall is the Mount?

Ⓐ 6

Ⓑ 5

Ⓒ 4

Ⓓ 3

20. Mrs. Jackson records the hair color of the 20 children in her room and obtains the following results:

Hair color	Number of students
Black	6
Brown	8
Blonde	4
Red	2

If the school has a total of 240 children, how many children with brown hair should be expected?

____

21. A grocery store determines the price of a gallon milk, *P*, in dollars will be determined by multiplying the wholesale price, *W*, in dollars by 1.5 and adding 25 cents. Which expression below represents this relationship?

Ⓐ $P = 1.5 + W + 0.25$

Ⓑ $P = 0.25W + 1.5$

Ⓒ $P = 1.75W$

Ⓓ $P = 1.5W + 0.25$

22. The movie Laura went to see ended at 8:15 PM. The movie she saw was 2 hours and 45 minutes long. What time did the movie start?

Ⓐ 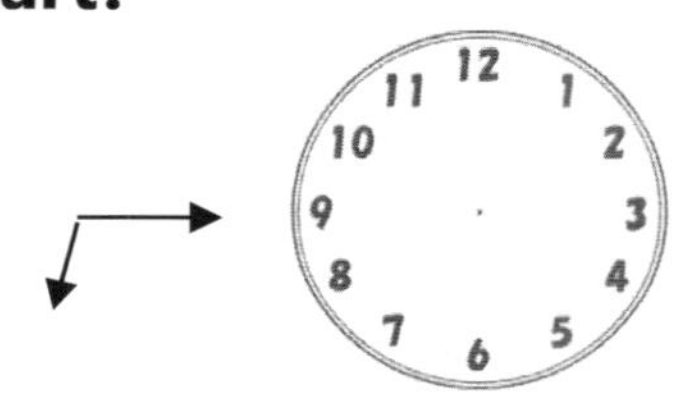

Ⓑ 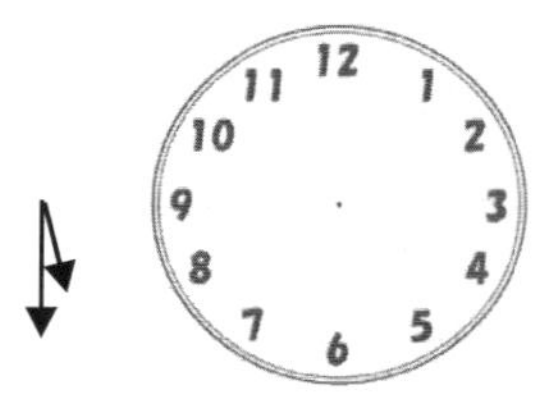

Ⓒ 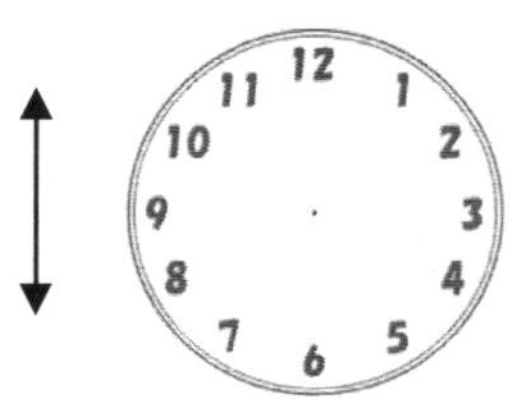

Ⓓ 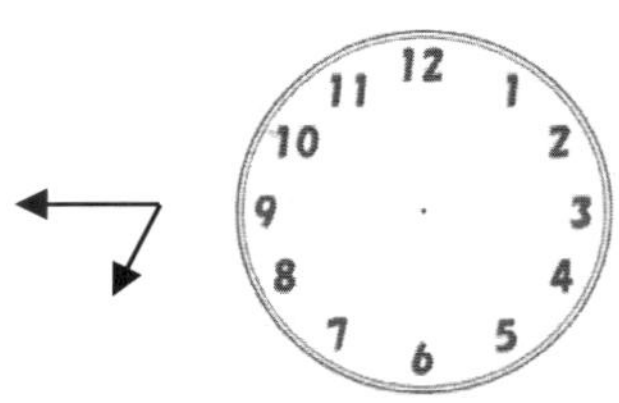

23. Using order of operations solve the problem below.

$3 + (9 - 4) \times (4 + 5) = ?$

____

24. On Saturday Allen spent 73 minutes mowing the grass. He spent 42 minutes washing his car, another 56 minutes repairing a fence, and 31 minutes trimming the shrubs. How much time did he spend doing chores on Saturday?

Ⓐ 2 hours 51 minutes
Ⓑ 3 hours 22 minutes
Ⓒ 3 hours 18 minutes
Ⓓ 3 hours 28 minutes

25. Which one of the statements about the rectangular prism below is FALSE?

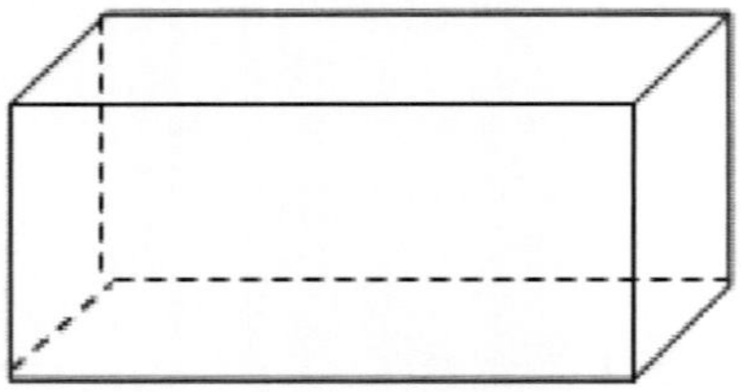

Ⓐ There are 12 edges on the rectangular prism.
Ⓑ The six sides of the rectangular prism all have the same area.
Ⓒ Some of the edges are parallel.
Ⓓ There are 8 vertices on the rectangular prism.

26. The model shown below represents $1\frac{5}{10}$

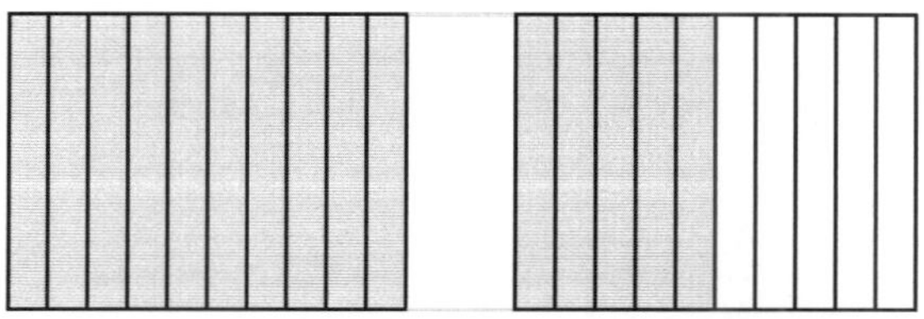

Which decimal does this also represent?

Ⓐ 0.5

Ⓑ 1.5

Ⓒ 1.05

Ⓓ 1.005

27. An observation tower is located at point (8, 5) on the map grid below. A fire is observed from a location 4 units west and 2 units north of the tower. What is the location of the fire?

Ⓐ (12, 7)

Ⓑ (4, 7)

Ⓒ (6, 9)

Ⓓ (4, 5)

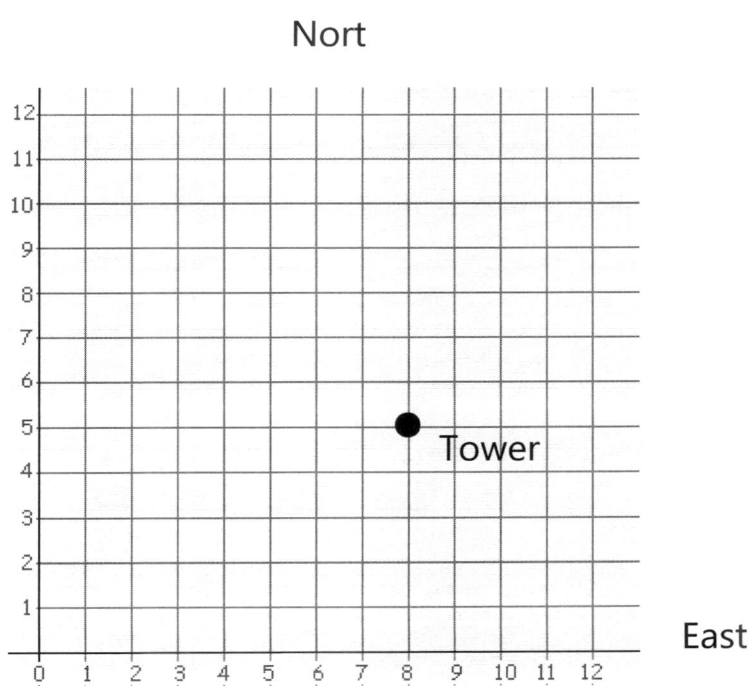

28. Maria is moving and needs a box to pack books in. The box needs to be 416 cubic inches. Which of the following boxes is the right size?

Ⓐ a box that is $8\ in. \times 12\ in. \times 5\ in.$

Ⓑ a box that is $12\ in. \times 4\ in. \times 9\ in.$

Ⓒ a box that is $13\ in. \times 5\ in. \times 7\ in.$

Ⓓ a box that is $13\ in. \times 4\ in. \times 8\ in.$

29. The number of washes the Squeaky Clean car wash made last week is given in the table below:

Day	Monday	Tuesday	Wednesday	Thursday	Friday
Car Washes	22	28	38	47	45

What is the mean number of car washes for the week?

Ⓐ 44

Ⓑ 47

Ⓒ 36

Ⓓ 31

30. 0.28 x 0.17

Ⓐ 0.2260

Ⓑ 0.4760

Ⓒ 0.0226

Ⓓ 0.0476

31. Jim brings two ice chests to the beach. Ice chest A has two compartments, while Ice Chest B just has one. Ice chest B can hold 24 drinks while Ice chest A can hold twice as many. If the larger compartment in Ice Chest A holds 34, how many does the smaller one hold?

____

32. Mandy's Farmer's Market sells pears in boxes of 18. A shipment of 417 pears arrives that morning. How many full boxes of pears can Mandy sell using that shipment?

Ⓐ 25

Ⓑ 23

Ⓒ 18

Ⓓ 20

33. The side length of a regular pentagon is 6.5 centimeters. What is the perimeter of this figure?

Ⓐ 26.0 cm.

Ⓑ 42.25 cm.

Ⓒ 39.0 cm.

Ⓓ 32.5 cm.

34. A length of yarn is measured to be $\frac{35}{8}$ inches. Between which points on the ruler will this length lie?

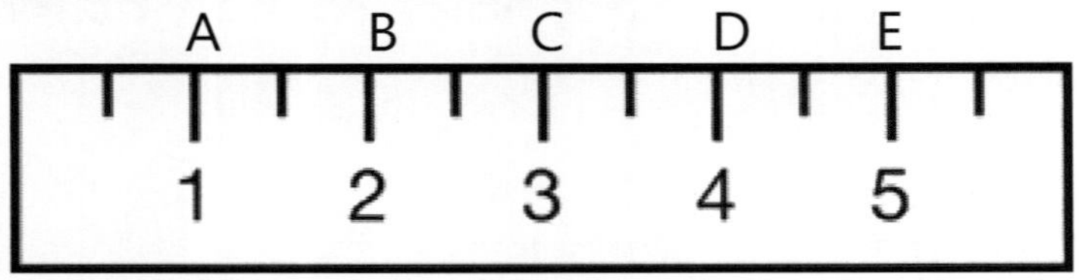

Ⓐ Between points A and B

Ⓑ Between points B and C

Ⓒ Between points C and D

Ⓓ Between points D and E

25. Which point lies within the shaded region below?

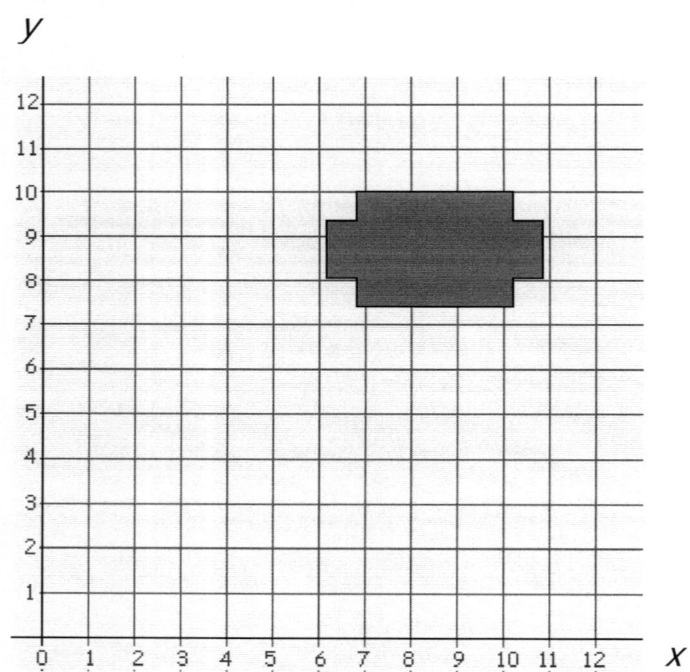

Ⓐ (5, 8)

Ⓑ (8, 9)

Ⓒ (7, 11)

Ⓓ (9, 7)

26. The workers at a large construction site were made up of 11 plumbers, 7 electricians, 13 carpenters, 8 concrete finishers and 11 laborers. What is the probability that a worker chosen at random will be either a carpenter or an electrician?

Ⓐ $\frac{13}{50}$

Ⓑ $\frac{9}{25}$

Ⓒ $\frac{2}{5}$

Ⓓ $\frac{7}{25}$

27. Which line graph correctly reflects the data shown in the table?

Time	Number of Customers
2:00 pm	20
4:00 pm	30
6:00 pm	50
8:00 pm	10

Ⓐ

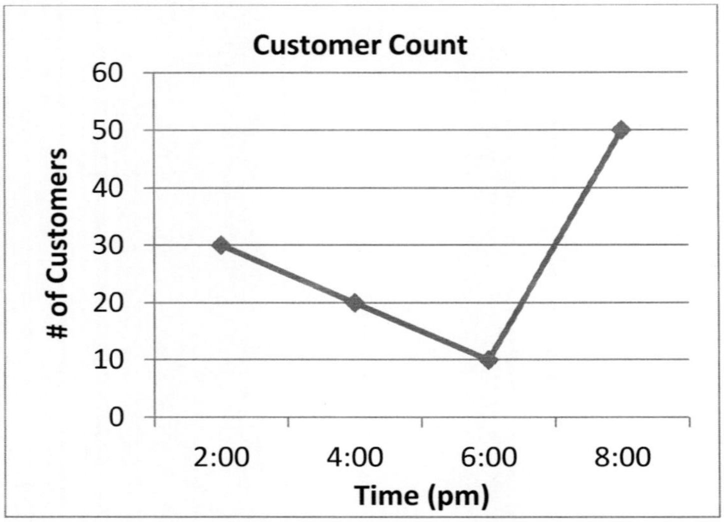

Ⓑ

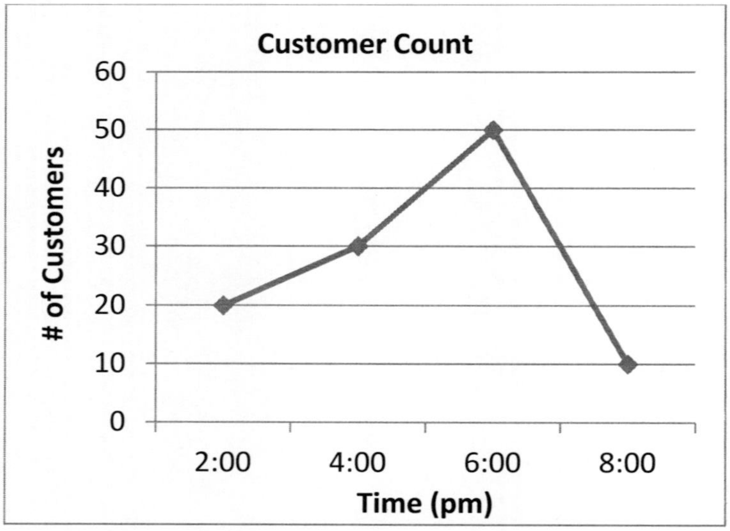

Ⓒ

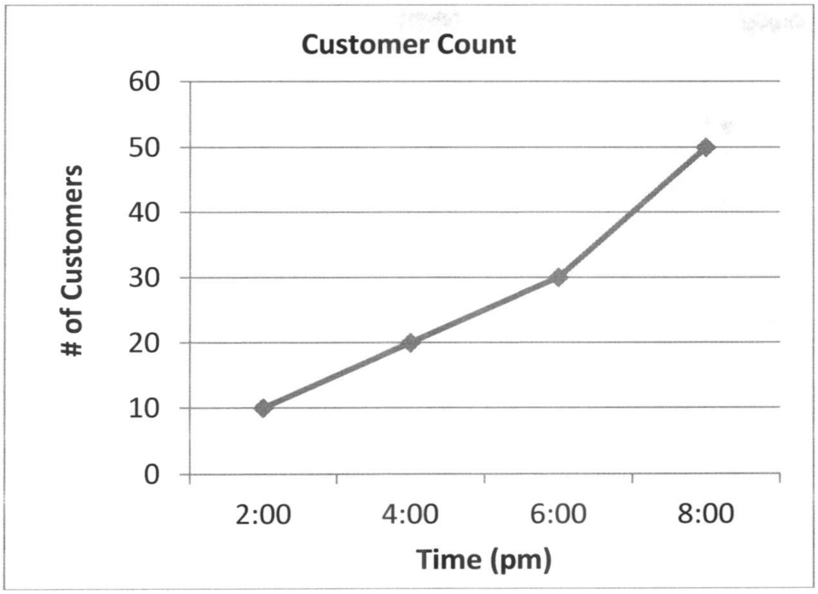
Customer Count
# of Customers
60
50
40
30
20
10
0
2:00
4:00
6:00
8:00
Time (pm)

Ⓓ

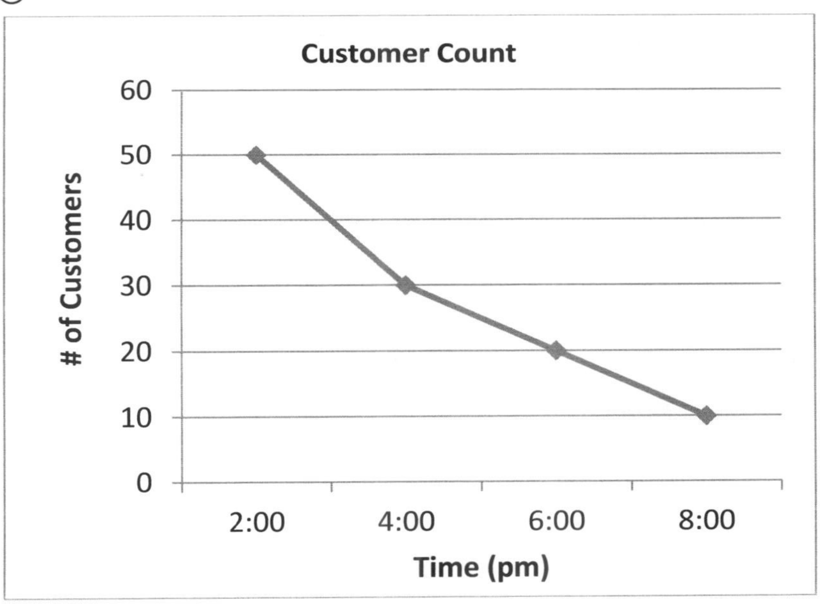
Customer Count
# of Customers
60
50
40
30
20
10
0
2:00
4:00
6:00
8:00
Time (pm)

28. Four students measured the length of the pencil each was using. The list shows the lengths, in centimeters, of the four pencils.

17.03 cm, 17.4 cm, 17.31 cm, 17.09 cm

Which list shows the lengths of the pencils in order, from shortest to longest?

Ⓐ *17.4 cm, 17.31 cm, 17.09 cm, 17.03 cm*

Ⓑ *17.03 cm, 17.09 cm, 17.4 cm, 17.31 cm*

Ⓒ *17.4 cm, 17.03 cm, 17.09 cm, 17.31 cm*

Ⓓ *17.03 cm, 17.09 cm, 17.31 cm, 17.4 cm*

29. What is the equivalent decimal number for five hundred twelve thousandths?

Ⓐ 0.512

Ⓑ 0.0512

Ⓒ 5120.

Ⓓ 0.00512

40. Reduce $\frac{14}{98}$ to lowest terms.

Ⓐ $\frac{7}{49}$

Ⓑ $\frac{2}{14}$

Ⓒ $\frac{1}{7}$

Ⓓ $\frac{3}{8}$

Thank You

We at Mometrix would like to extend our heartfelt thanks to you, our friend and patron, for allowing us to play a part in your journey. It is a privilege to serve people from all walks of life who are unified in their commitment to building the best future they can for themselves.

The preparation you devote to these important testing milestones may be the most valuable educational opportunity you have for making a real difference in your life. We encourage you to put your heart into it—that feeling of succeeding, overcoming, and yes, conquering will be well worth the hours you've invested.

We want to hear your story, your struggles and your successes, and if you see any opportunities for us to improve our materials so we can help others even more effectively in the future, please share that with us as well. **The team at Mometrix would be absolutely thrilled to hear from you!** So please, send us an email (support@mometrix.com) and let's stay in touch.

Online Resources

Due to our efforts to try to keep this book to a manageable length, we've created a link that will give you access to all of your online resources:

mometrix.com/resources719/ssmstepg5mathwb

It's Your Moment, Let's Celebrate It!

Share your story @mometrixtestpreparation